50% OFF

Online MASS Prep Course!

Dear Customer,

Thank you for your purchase of this Power Plant Maintenance Positions Selection System (MASS) Study Guide. Included with your purchase is **discounted access to our online MASS Prep Course**. Many MASS courses are needlessly expensive and don't deliver enough value. Our course provides the best MASS prep material, and with discounted access, **you only pay half price**.

We have structured our online course to perfectly complement your printed study guide. The MASS Prep Course contains **in-depth lessons** that cover all the most important topics, **20+ video reviews** that explain difficult concepts, and over **350 practice questions** to ensure you feel prepared, so you can study while you're on the go.

Online MASS Prep Course

Topics Included:

- Assembling Objects
- Mechanical Concepts
  - Kinematics
  - Kinetics
  - Work/Energy
  - Machines
  - Momentum/Impulse
  - And more!
- Reading Comprehension
- Mathematical Usage
- Background and Opinion Questionnaire

Course Features:

- MASS Study Guide
  - Get content that complements our best-selling study guide.
- Full-Length Practice Tests
  - With over 350 practice questions, you can test yourself again and again.
- Mobile Friendly
  - If you need to study on the go, the course is easily accessible from your mobile device.

To lock in your discounted access, visit mometrix.com/university/mass or simply scan this QR code with your smartphone. At the checkout page, enter the discount code: **mass50off**

If you have any questions or concerns, please contact us at support@mometrix.com.

Mometrix
TEST PREPARATION

Power Plant Maintenance Selection System Practice Questions

Mometrix

TEST PREPARATION

Dear Future Exam Success Story

First of all, **THANK YOU** for purchasing Mometrix study materials!

Second, congratulations! You are one of the few determined test-takers who are committed to doing whatever it takes to excel on your exam. **You have come to the right place.** We developed these practice tests with one goal in mind: to deliver you the best possible approximation of the questions you will see on test day.

Standardized testing is one of the biggest obstacles on your road to success, which only increases the importance of doing well in the high-pressure, high-stakes environment of test day. Your results on this test could have a significant impact on your future, and these practice tests will give you the repetitions you need to build your familiarity and confidence with the test content and format to help you achieve your full potential on test day.

Your success is our success

We would love to hear from you! If you would like to share the story of your exam success or if you have any questions or comments in regard to our products, please contact us at **800-673-8175** or **support@mometrix.com**.

Thanks again for your business and we wish you continued success!

Sincerely,
The Mometrix Test Preparation Team

Written and edited by the Mometrix Exam Secrets Test Prep Team
Printed in the United States of America

Table of Contents

Practice Test #1

Mathematical Usage

Use the following information to answer questions 1-18:

1 acre	=	43,560 square feet
1 barrel	=	42 gallons
1 fathom	=	6 feet
1 foot	=	12 inches
1 furlong	=	40 rods
1 gallon	=	3.785 liters
1 gallon	=	4 quarts
1 hand	=	10 centimeters
1 inch	=	2.54 centimeters
1 kilogram	=	1,000 grams
1 kilogram	=	2.2 pounds
1 kilometer	=	1,000 meters
1 mile	=	1.609 kilometers
1 mile	=	5,280 feet
3 mile/hour	=	4.4 feet/second
1 pint	=	4 gills
1 pound	=	16 ounces
1 quart	=	2 pints
1 slug	=	14.59 kilograms
1 square mile	=	640 acres

If none of the answers listed are correct, select answer e, N for none of the above.

1. 1 quart = ? gallons

a. 0.25
b. 0.33
c. 4
d. 5
e. N

2. 60 rods = ? furlongs

a. 0.1
b. 0.5
c. 1.5
d. 2,400
e. N

3. 2 slugs = ? grams

a. 7.295
b. 29.18
c. 4,000
d. 29,180
e. N

4. 87,120 square feet = ? acres

a. 0.5
b. 1
c. 2
d. 43,560
e. N

5. 4 miles = ? kilometers

a. 1.243
b. 1.609
c. 2.486
d. 6.436
e. N

6. 0.5 pounds = ? ounces

a. 5
b. 8
c. 12
d. 80
e. N

7. 12 feet = ? fathoms

a. 2
b. 6
c. 12
d. 72
e. N

8. 2 barrels = ? gallons

a. 21
b. 42
c. 84
d. 92
e. N

9. 4 kilograms = ? pounds

a. 2.2
b. 4.4
c. 8.8
d. 17.6
e. N

10. 5 kilograms = ? grams

a. 0.05
b. 0.5
c. 50
d. 5,000
e. N

11. 5 hands = ? centimeters

a. 0.5
b. 1.5
c. 38
d. 50
e. N

12. 17.6 feet/second = ? miles/hour

a. 4
b. 8
c. 12
d. 17.6
e. N

13. 1 barrel = ? quarts

a. 21
b. 168
c. 336
d. 672
e. N

14. 5,280 inches = ? miles

a. $\frac{1}{12}$
b. 1
c. 12
d. 13,411
e. N

15. 2 feet = ? hands

a. 2
b. 6.096
c. 10
d. 4,028
e. N

16. 7 pints = ? gallons

a. 0.75
b. 1.5
c. 3
d. 6
e. N

17. 16 quarts = ? liters

a. 0.53
b. 7.57
c. 15.14
d. 121.12
e. N

18. 4 feet = ? centimeters

a. 23.61
b. 60
c. 121.92
d. 152.40
e. N

Reading for Comprehension

Passage #1

Deposits of fossil fuels are scattered around the world. There are some regions of the world that have rich and plentiful deposits, while other regions have none at all. The location of fossil fuel deposits depends on a number of factors.

Coal is made up of the remains of swamp plants that were alive hundreds of millions of years ago. When these plant remains are covered by layers of sediment and then compressed within the crust of the earth, there is the potential for deposits to form. Between 250 and 300 million years ago, large swaths of the eastern United States were swampy, which explains the rich coal deposits that are found there today. There are also coal deposits in the western United States, though these are only around a hundred million years old.

Oil and natural gas are the products of decaying marine organisms. The marine organisms that compose the deposits being mined today were alive millions of years ago. The marine organisms died, and their remains were covered by sediment. Beneath the surface of the earth, the heat and pressure gradually converted them into complex carbon molecules. In places where the carbon deposits were alongside formations of porous rock, the molecules seeped into this rock. These days, the largest deposits of oil and natural gas in the United States are found in Alaska, Texas, California, and underneath the Gulf of Mexico.

Finding these deposits of oil and natural gas has become an incredibly sophisticated and expensive process. Experts have discovered that oil and natural gas tends to settle in certain geological arrangements, like salt domes and faults, where there is a space enclosed by impermeable rock. Unless there is a border of nonporous rock, the oil and natural gas will be distributed over a much larger area, which will make it more difficult to access. Once geologists have identified a promising area, they will drill exploratory wells to obtain more information about the deposits there. Sometimes, the exploratory wells indicate that the oil or natural gas is not plentiful, or will be difficult to extract. If the wells deliver positive feedback, however, larger wells will be drilled so that more of the fossil fuels can be pumped to the surface. In its raw state, this oil is known as petroleum. Before it can be used by consumers and in industry, petroleum must be refined at special facilities.

1. What is the source of oil and natural gas?

a. Decaying marine organisms
b. Oil derricks
c. Decaying swamp plants
d. Coal deposits

2. What is the subject of the third paragraph?

a. The sources of fossil fuels
b. The process of drilling exploratory wells
c. The sources of oil and natural gas deposits
d. The locations of coal deposits

3. The raw oil pumped to the surface of an oil well is called:

a. Carbon
b. Petroleum
c. Natural gas
d. Coal

4. Based on the information in the passage, which of the following statements is probably true?

a. In a few hundred million years, there will be rich coal deposits underneath the Dakotas.
b. Petroleum is dangerous to touch.
c. The western United States is still covered by swamps.
d. Exploratory wells are less expensive than full-scale wells.

5. Why are there rich coal deposits in the eastern United States?

a. Because this area was swampy millions of years ago
b. Because of the animals that lived there millions of years ago
c. Because of the climate
d. Because of the rock formations

6. Which of the following questions does the passage focus on answering?

a. Why are the supplies of fossil fuels limited?
b. Where do fossil fuels come from?
c. Where are the best deposits of oil and natural gas?
d. How are fossil fuels found?

7. Why are useful oil deposits typically surrounded by impermeable rock?

a. Oil is created by some types of impermeable rock.
b. Otherwise, they will seep into the rocks around them.
c. Permeable rocks tend to pollute the oil supply.
d. Impermeable rock is more common below the surface of the earth.

Passage #2

Breeder reactors were developed as a solution to the scarcity of uranium. This was particularly worrisome back in the 1960s, when there was more optimism about nuclear power. Breeder reactors are useful, because they maximize the isotopes used in the production of nuclear power. However, these reactors pose some unique challenges to engineers and safety personnel.

A standard nuclear reactor requires an isotope of uranium, U^{235}. During fission, two or three neutrons will be ejected from each atom of U^{235}. However, all but one of these neutrons will be absorbed and will not perform their intended function of knocking another neutron loose from another atom. In a breeder reactor, the U^{235} is combined with U^{238}, in which fission does not take place. The extra neutrons will be absorbed by the U^{238}, which will then become plutonium, specifically Pu^{239}. This form of plutonium can be used as nuclear fuel. Therefore, since, multiple neutrons are dislodged in the fission of U^{235}, a breeder reactor may be able to generate more fuel than it consumes.

At present, there are two main types of breeder reactor. A fast breeder reactor, commonly known as an FBR, converts U^{238} into plutonium, though in some cases it can also create U^{233} from a less common fuel, the element thorium. This type of reactor uses so-called "fast" neutrons, which must be slowed down with a neutron moderator so that they can sustain a chain reaction. A thermal breeder reactor, meanwhile, only creates U^{233} from thorium. This type of reactor generates slower neutrons, which do not require moderation.

The appeal of breeder reactors is clear: they generate power without depleting uranium reserves. Unfortunately, breeder reactors also present some special risks. The plutonium used in a breeder reactor has a much longer half-life than U^{235}, so a meltdown would be much more catastrophic. Breeder reactors are very expensive to construct, operate, and maintain, as well. In addition, the plutonium used in breeder reactors is more readily convertible to weapons material. This means that breeder reactor facilities must be guarded closely.

Indeed, as the demand for new nuclear reactors has declined, and the concern over limited supplies of uranium has diminished, breeder reactors have mostly been used for military purposes. The United States is one of many countries that maintain breeder reactors strictly for the development of weapons-grade plutonium. Commercial use of breeder reactors has largely been restricted to Russia, Japan, and France. Even in these countries, breeder reactors have not been in continuous use.

8. According to the article, what is the primary advantage of breeder reactors?

a. They are less expensive to build.
b. They create less environmental damage.
c. They create endless chain reactions.
d. They use up less fuel.

9. In a breeder reactor, some of the uranium is converted into:

a. Natural gas
b. Carbon
c. Neutrons
d. Plutonium

10. What is the main reason for the decline in concern about limited supplies of uranium?

a. Diminished interest in building new nuclear power plants
b. Discovery of new deposits of uranium
c. Decline in the price of uranium in global markets
d. Development of more efficient technologies

11. Which of the following countries does not use breeder reactors for commercial purposes?

a. France
b. United States
c. Russia
d. Japan

12. Which type of breeder reactor requires thorium as fuel?

a. Fast breeder reactor
b. Instant breeder reactor
c. Thermal breeder reactor
d. Standard breeder reactor

13. Why would a meltdown in a breeder reactor be worse than a meltdown in a standard nuclear reactor?

a. Because breeder reactors are made of more flammable material
b. Because many breeder reactors are operated by unstable regimes
c. Because the plutonium in a breeder reactor has an extremely long half-life
d. Because breeder reactors are much more difficult to operate

14. Why does a fast breeder reactor need to include a neutron moderator?

a. To sustain the chain reaction
b. To accelerate the chain reaction
c. To end the chain reaction
d. To initiate the chain reaction

Passage #3

One of the more common facilities for the production of electricity is the gas turbine power plant. In a gas turbine power plant, the turbine is moved by the expansion of gasoline inside. The gasoline expands when it is heated. The gas turbine power plant is similar to a steam power plant, in which gasoline is burned to heat water, which turns into steam and expand inside the turbine. The gas turbine power plant simplifies this process by placing the gasoline inside the turbine itself, eliminating the need for water altogether.

Gas turbine power plants have a number of advantages. To begin with, they are easy to design and install. These systems are extremely reliable and do not cost much to build, relative to other power plant types. Gas turbine power plants are also quite compact: they do not need to be housed in large buildings, and they do not require a great deal of water for cooling. Moreover, gas turbine plants can be started and stopped quickly, and can move from a state of inaction to working at full capacity almost instantly. These power plants may be operated from a remote location, and require very few maintenance personnel while the plant is at work. Despite the fact that these plants consume more fuel than other types of power plant, they almost never require expensive repairs or maintenance.

There are, however, some drawbacks to the gas turbine power plant. The major disadvantage of these plants is that they produce little net output relative to their consumption of fuel. In a gas turbine power plant, the bulk of the fuel consumption goes toward powering the compressor, and a great deal of heat is lost through the exhaust gases. Another disadvantage of the gas turbine power plant is that it may only be powered with lighter petroleum products: in other words, coal and other heavy residual petroleum products cannot be used. Gas turbine electric power plants are loud, and they can only produce a limited amount of electricity.

Some of the problems of gas turbine power plants are in the process of being resolved. For instance, scientists are attempting to make these plants more efficient by installing regenerators, intercoolers, and reheaters. A regenerator uses the heat of the exhaust gases to warm the compressed air before it enters the combustion chamber, which diminishes the amount of power needed to operate the plant. An intercooler cools the compressed air between the stages of compression, thus improving the work ratio, thermal efficiency, and air rate. A reheater further expands gases that have already been partially expanded in the turbine; this process is especially beneficial for plants that have a moderate cycle temperature.

15. Which of the following is NOT an advantage of the gas turbine power plant?

a. Gas turbine power plants are inexpensive to construct.
b. Gas turbine power plants do not require a great deal of water for cooling.
c. Gas turbine power plants do not require large buildings.
d. Gas turbine power plants retain almost all of their heat energy.

16. Which piece of equipment chills the compressed air in between compression stages?

a. Intercooler
b. Turbine
c. Regenerator
d. Reheater

17. The third paragraph of the passage deals primarily with:

a. The latest innovations for gas turbine power plants
b. The disadvantages of gas turbine power plants
c. The environmental impact of gas turbine power plants
d. The positive aspects of gas turbine power plants

18. Which of the following statements about gas turbine power plants is true?

a. A regenerator increases the amount of fuel needed to operate a gas turbine power plant.
b. Gas turbine power plants can use coal as fuel.
c. It takes a long time for gas turbine power plants to change speed.
d. Gas turbine power plants operate in much the same way as steam power plants.

19. What does a regenerator do?

a. Heats up compressed air before it enters the combustion chamber
b. Replenishes the supply of natural gas
c. Cools compressed air between compression stages
d. Increases the amount of power required for plant operation

20. Based on the information presented in the passage, which aspect of gas turbine power plants needs the most improvement?

a. Cost
b. Efficiency
c. Environmental impact
d. Design

Passage #4

Electricity is referred to as a secondary energy source, because it must be derived from another, primary source. For instance, many power plants burn coal or use waterpower to turn a generator, which creates the electricity. About a third of the fossil fuel production in the United States goes to the creation of electricity.

There are a few different methods for converting primary energy sources into electricity. The most basic of these is the generator, which was invented in the nineteenth century. The development of the first generators was based on a simple observation: when a coil of wire is passed through a magnetic field, an electrical current moves through the wire. This electrical current is the flow of electrons. A simple generator just rotates a coil of wire in a magnetic field (or, conversely, rotates the magnetic field around the coil). In this way, mechanical energy becomes electricity.

These simple generators create a great deal of waste. To begin with, they lose energy through heat and whatever friction exists in the workings of the machine. In addition, the current that flows through the wire creates its own magnetic field, which will be opposed to the first field and therefore, to the flow of the current. In electrical production, the general rule is that it takes three units of primary energy to create one unit of electricity. However, electricity is valuable enough for this to be worthwhile.

A slightly more complicated, but also more powerful system for generating electrical power is the turbogenerator, so named, because it combines a turbine with a generator. A turbogenerator works by using a primary energy source to boil water, which produces steam in a confined space: the resulting pressure is enough to spin the turbine. The most common primary energy sources for turbogenerators are coal, oil, and nuclear power, but researchers are at work to develop more environmentally friendly sources.

Some turbogenerators do not require steam for their operation. A hydroelectric turbine uses water that is under great pressure, typically because it is at the bottom of a dam or a long pipe. A gas turbogenerator uses the tremendous heat generated by the combustion of natural gas to drive the turbine. There is also an ongoing effort to develop wind turbines that can efficiently produce large amounts of power.

21. Which of the following would be the best title for this passage?

a. "Simple Generators"
b. "The Value of Electricity"
c. "The Production of Electricity"
d. "Primary Energy Sources"

22. Based on the information in the passage, which action would increase the efficiency of a simple generator?

a. Lubricating the parts
b. Rotating the coil by hand
c. Increasing the power
d. Venting the steam

23. The third paragraph of this passage describes:

a. The ways in which a traditional generator loses energy
b. The operation of a turbogenerator
c. The next generation of turbines
d. The development of the first generators

24. How much of the fossil fuel production in the United States goes to the production of electricity?

a. 1/4
b. 1/3
c. 1/2
d. 2/3

25. Based on the information provided in the passage, which of the following statements is false?

a. Simple generators lose a great deal of energy through heat.
b. The magnetic field created by an electrical current is opposed to the flow of the current.
c. There are a few different types of hydroelectric turbine.
d. Simple generators are more powerful than turbogenerators.

26. Which of the following is NOT one of the common primary energy sources for turbogenerators?

a. Nuclear power
b. Steam
c. Coal
d. Oil

27. Why are turbogenerators called that?

a. Because they require special fuel
b. Because they are much faster than normal generators
c. Because they harness the power of automobile engines
d. Because they combine a turbine with a generator

28. Based on the information in the passage, which of the following statements is probably true?

a. Wind turbines are inefficient at present.
b. Turbogenerators must have steam in order to operate.
c. Electrical energy is less valuable than heat energy.
d. Turbogenerators were developed in the nineteenth century.

Passage #5

The demand for new nuclear plants in the United States has declined over the past few decades, in part because of the diminishing economic results of these facilities. There are a few reasons for this decline in demand. To begin with, forecasters in the 1960s and 1970s drastically overestimated the amount of energy that would be required by Americans in the coming decades, which meant that more new power plants were built than were needed. This has diminished demand for every type of power plant.

Another reason why fewer nuclear power plants have been built is that disasters like Three Mile Island and Chernobyl aroused public skepticism of nuclear power plants, and so every new plant proposal was met with protests. This discouraged investment and delayed construction, which increased the start-up costs. When start-up costs increase, so do utility bills for the consumers who ultimately receive the power. Higher utility bills increase public dissatisfaction with nuclear power, and the demand for more plants is diminished further.

The high-profile catastrophes had another consequence for future nuclear development: stricter safety standards, which require greater outlays during construction and operation. Some analysts estimate that the cost of building and maintaining a nuclear power plant has more than quadrupled because of increased regulation. At the same time, the United States government has been less willing to subsidize an unpopular industry, so utility companies have had to bear the costs of new plants alone.

A final driver of costs for nuclear power plants has been the shorter-than-expected lifespan of the plants that already exist. In the heyday of nuclear plant construction, it was believed that these plants would last about forty years, but, in practice, they have only lasted an average of seventeen. The scientists who oversaw the construction of the first plants did not know that steady bombardment by neutrons would weaken the reactor vessel, a process known as embrittlement, or that corrosive chemicals would gradually degrade the pipes used for generating steam.

No matter the cause, when plants operate for less than half of their anticipated lives, the power they produce becomes much more expensive. Shutting these plants down can be quite expensive, as well. This process, known as decommissioning, can run into the hundreds of millions of dollars and is often much more than the cost of building the plant in the first place. In some cases, the facilities can be converted into natural gas power plants, but there are many former nuclear plants that sit idle for years as owners struggle to cover the costs of properly disposing of material and equipment.

29. What would be the best title for this passage?

a. "The Rise of Nuclear Power"
b. "Nuclear Power: Rising Costs and Declining Demand"
c. "The Dangers of Nuclear Power"
d. "Nuclear Power Plant: Operations and Maintenance"

30. What is the average life span of a nuclear power plant?

a. 10 years
b. 17 years
c. 26 years
d. 40 years

31. Why has the United States government been less willing to subsidize the construction of new nuclear power plants?

a. Because nuclear power plants are dangerous
b. Because nuclear power plants are expensive
c. Because nuclear power plants are unpopular
d. Because nuclear power plants are less durable than expected

32. What is the main idea of the fourth paragraph in this passage?

a. Nuclear power plants have not lasted as long as expected.
b. A few major disasters have decreased demand for new nuclear reactors.
c. The corrosion of pipes has made it difficult to generate steam.
d. Nuclear power plants should be decommissioned.

33. What is embrittlement?

a. The corrosion of the pipes used to generate steam
b. The disposal of the hazardous waste generated by a nuclear power plant
c. The closing of nuclear power plants
d. Degradation of the reactor vessel by continuous neutron bombardment

34. Which of the following cost drivers has resulted from nuclear disasters like Three Mile Island?

a. Increased safety requirements
b. Lower government subsidies
c. Longer construction times
d. All of the above

35. Based on the information in thc passage, which of the following is true?

a. The construction of nuclear power plants in the 1960s and 70s decreased the demand for gas turbine power plants.
b. Protests against nuclear power have decreased utility costs for consumers.
c. It is more economical to decommission failing nuclear power plants than to build new ones.
d. Americans are using less electricity than was expected decades ago.

36. Why are nuclear power plants so costly to shut down?

a. Because they have to be decommissioned
b. Because a new plant must be opened in the same location
c. Because special equipment must be purchased
d. Because disposing of radioactive material is very expensive

Assembling Objects

For this practice test section, assume that shapes may be rotated but not reflected.

1. Which of the following configurations represents how the following objects might appear if they are rearranged?

a. 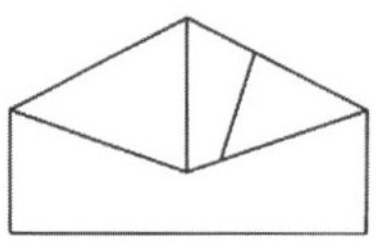 b. 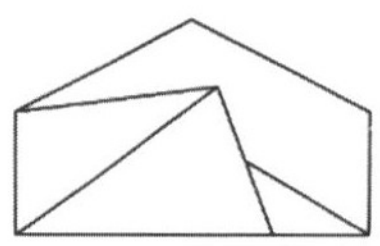 c. 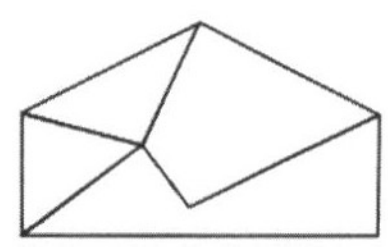 d. 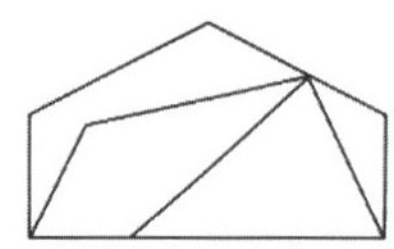

2. Which of the following configurations represents how the following objects might appear if they are rearranged?

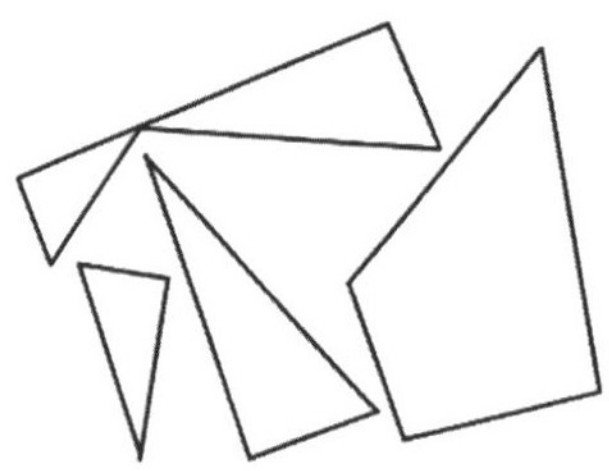

a. 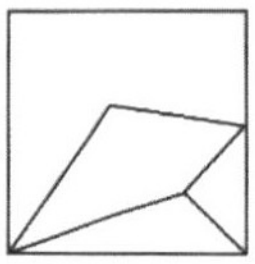 b. 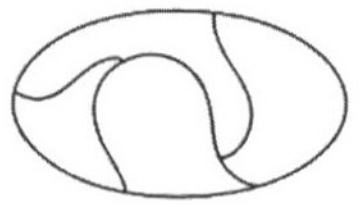 c. 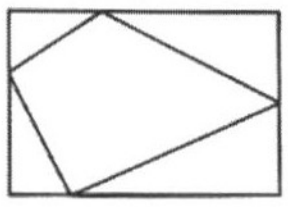 d. 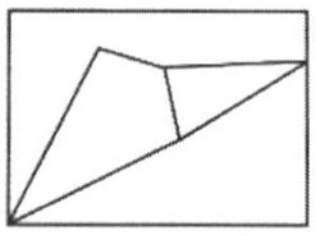

3. Which of the following configurations represents how the following object might appear if its components are rearranged?

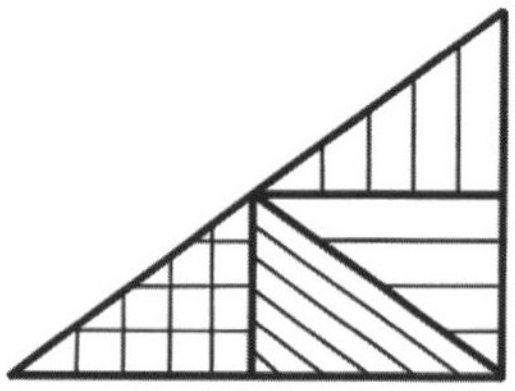

a. 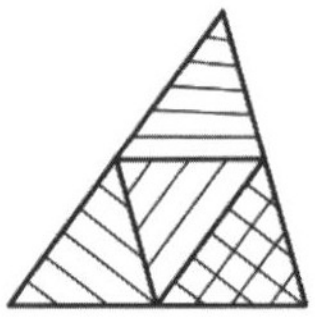 b. 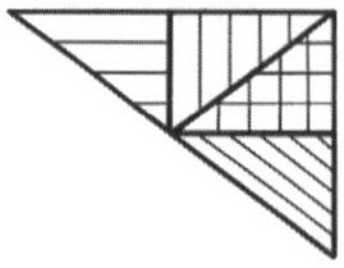 c. 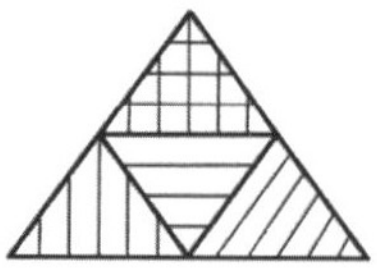 d. 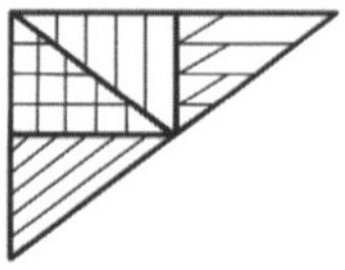

4. Which of the following configurations represents how the following objects might appear if they are rearranged?

a. 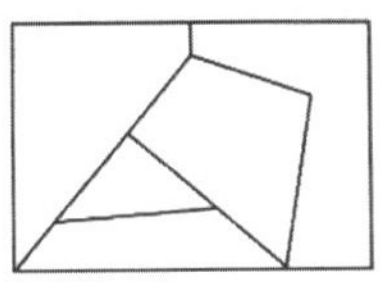 b. 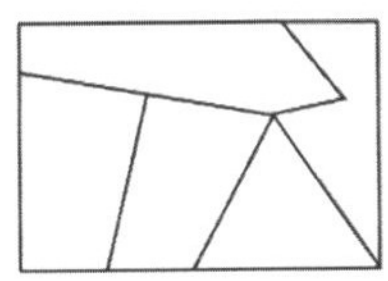 c. 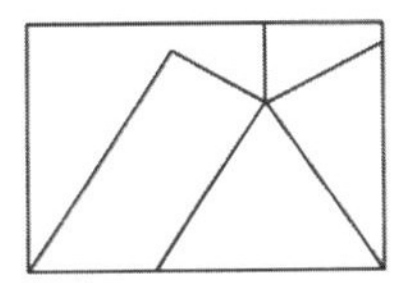 d. 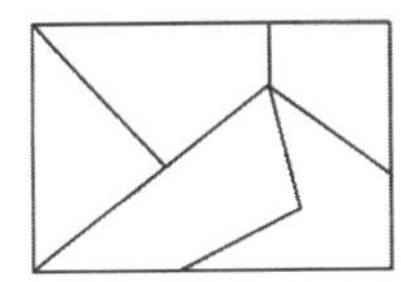

5. Which figure best shows what would happen if the triangle is placed directly on top of the rectangle shown without rotating either shape?

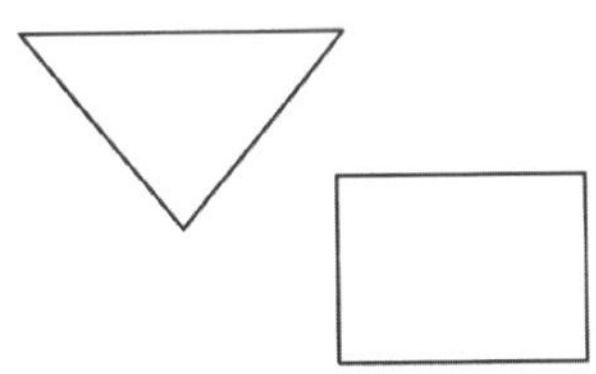

a.  b.  c. 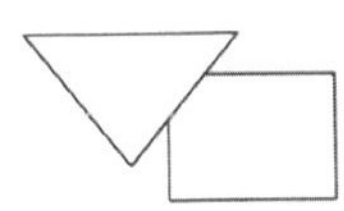 d. 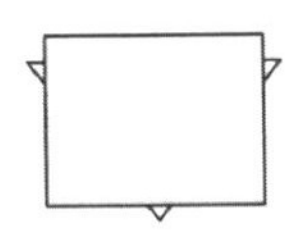

6. Which of the following configurations represents how the following object might appear if its components are rearranged?

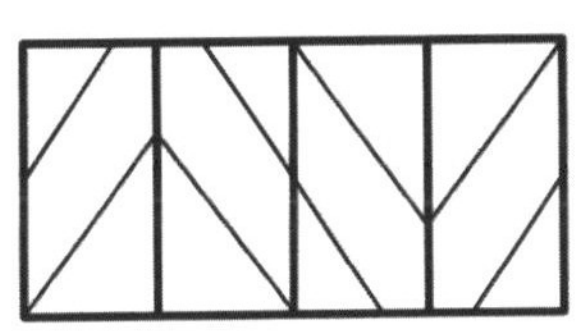

a. 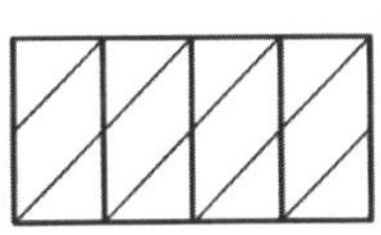 b. 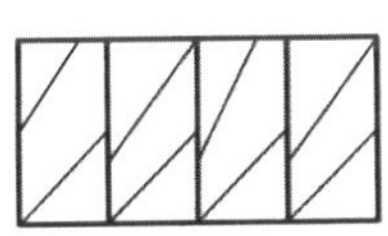 c. 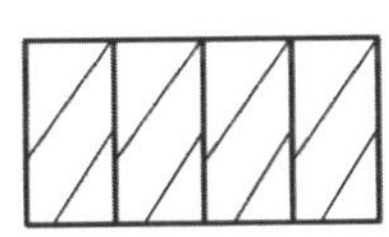 d. 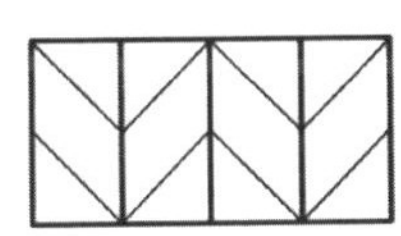

7. Which of the following configurations represents how the following objects might appear if they are rearranged?

a. 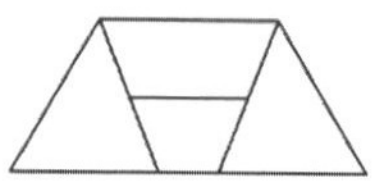 b. 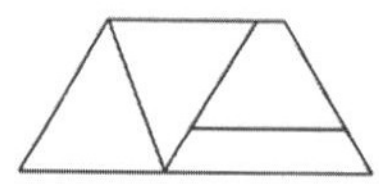 c. 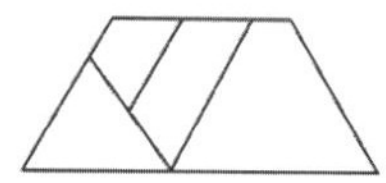 d. 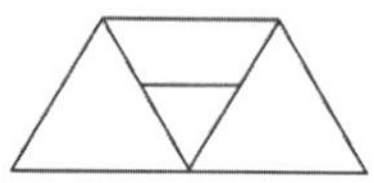

8. Which figure is a horizontal reflection or flip of the object shown?

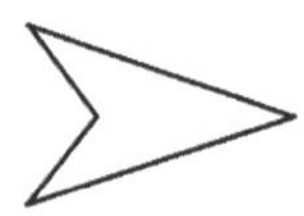

a.  b. 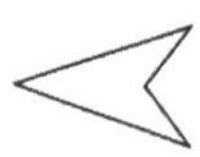 c.  d. 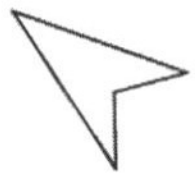

9. Which of the following configurations represents how the following objects might appear if they are rearranged?

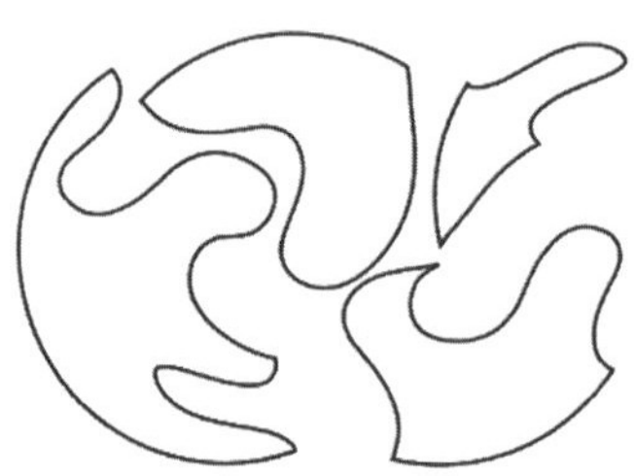

a.  b.  c.  d. 

10. If the objects below are translated along the path indicated by the line, keeping in mind that a dotted line corresponds to a place on the side of the object that cannot be seen, how might the final image appear? (Note: the images may not be rotated.)

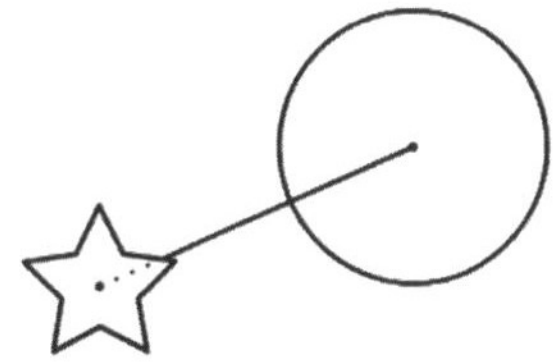

a. 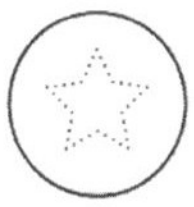 b.  c. 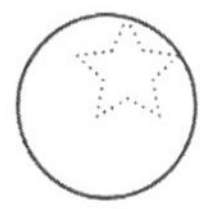 d. 

11. Which figure best shows what would happen if the smaller circles are aligned on top of each other?

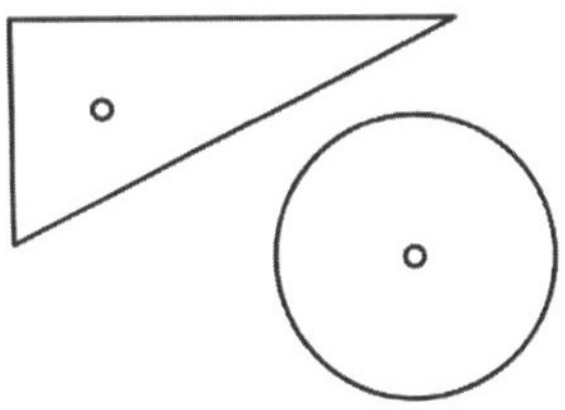

a. 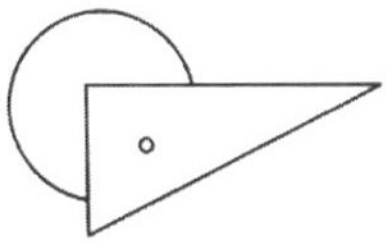 b. 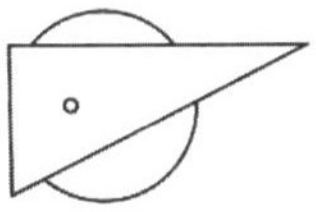 c. 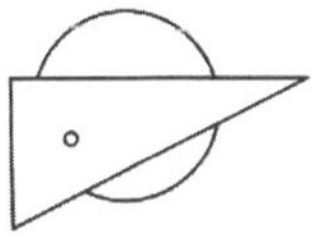 d. 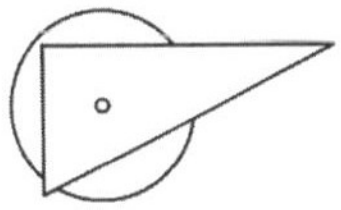

12. Which of the following configurations represents how the following objects might appear if they are rearranged?

a. 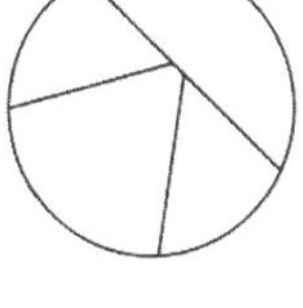 b. 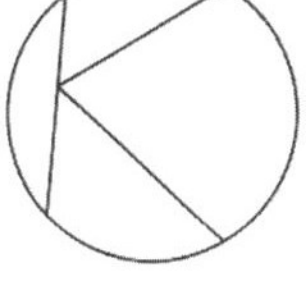 c. 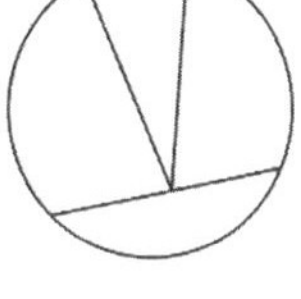 d. 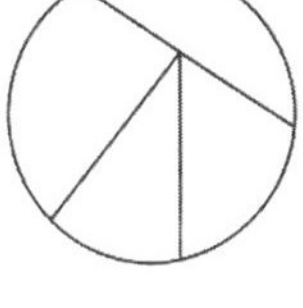

13. Which of the following configurations represents how the following object might appear if its components are rearranged?

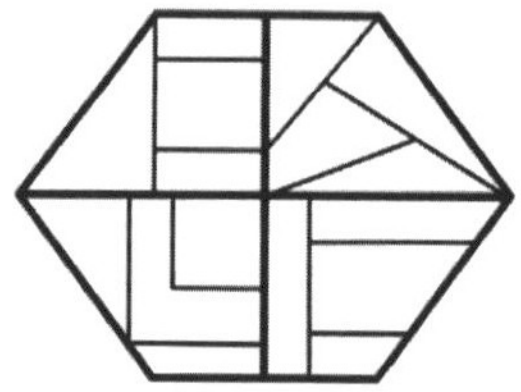

a. 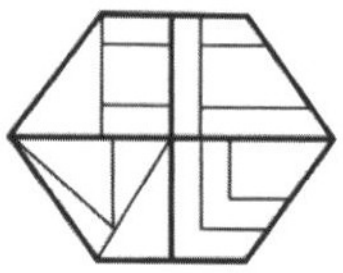 b. 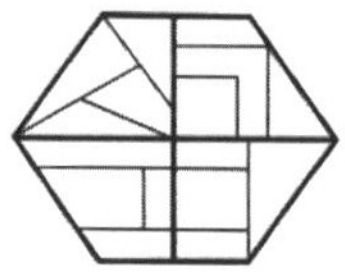 c. 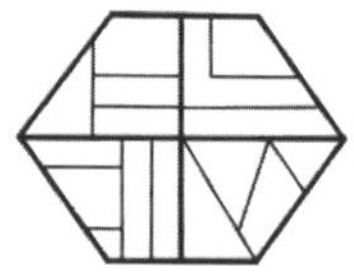 d. 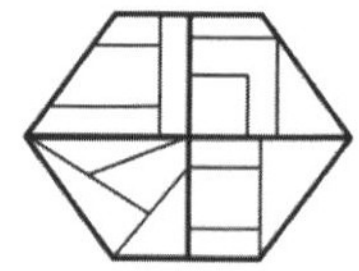

14. Which figure best represents what might result if the shapes shown on the left are cut out of the shape on the right?

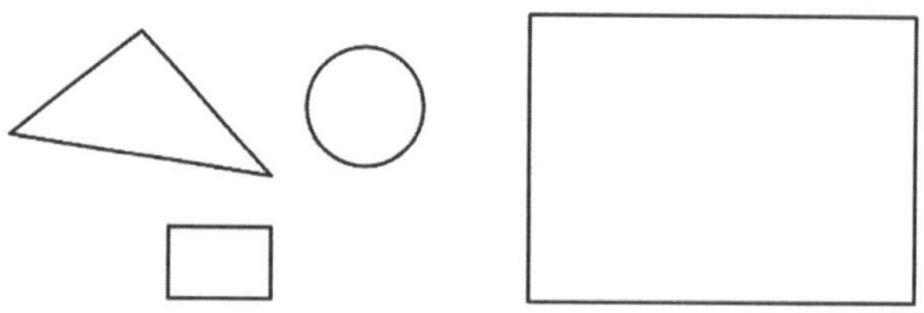

a. 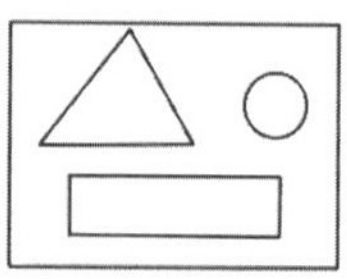 b. 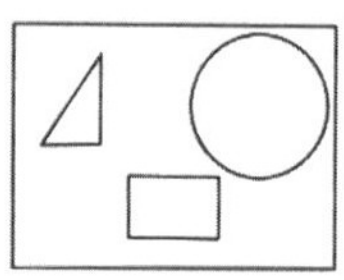 c. 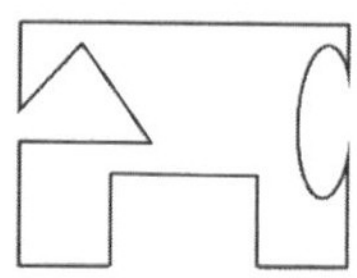 d. 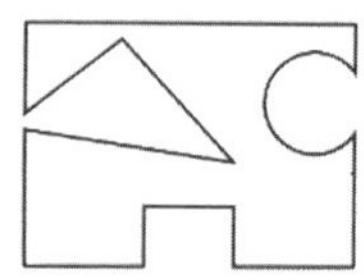

15. Which of the following configurations represents how the following objects might appear if they are rearranged?

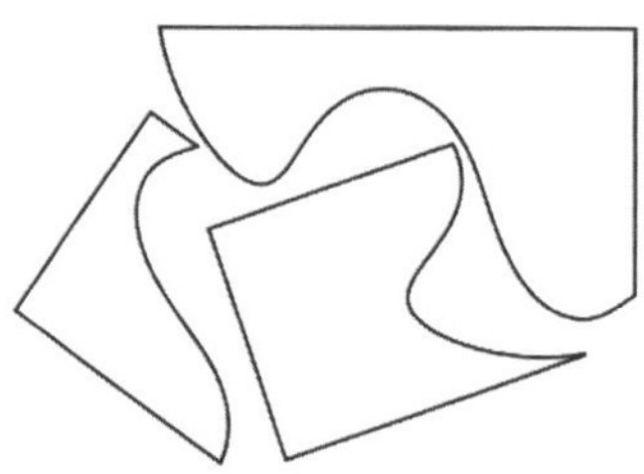

a. 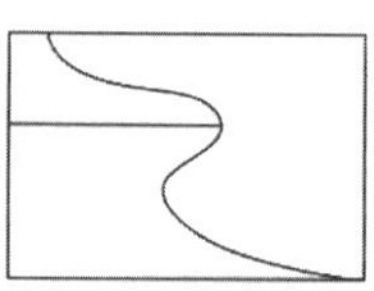 b. 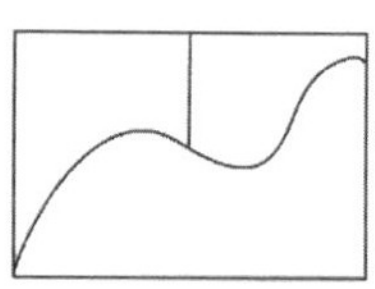 c. 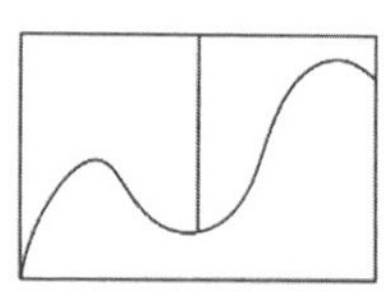 d. 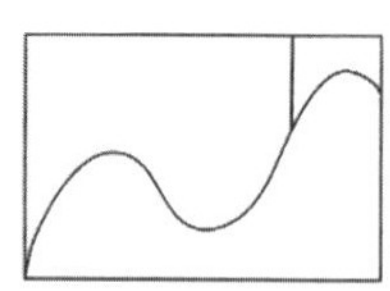

16. Which of the following configurations represents how the following object might appear if its components are rearranged?

a.  b.  c.  d. 

17. Which of the following configurations represents how the following objects might appear if they are rearranged?

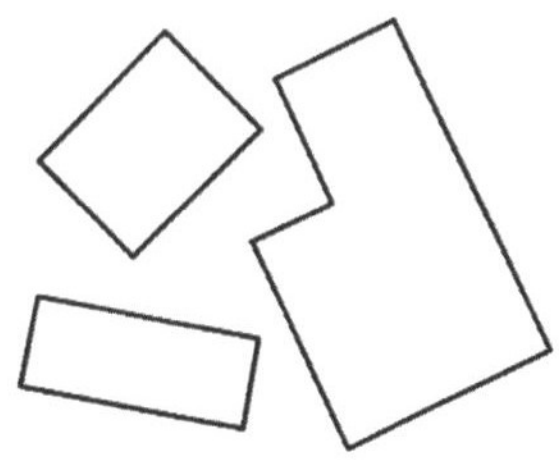

a. 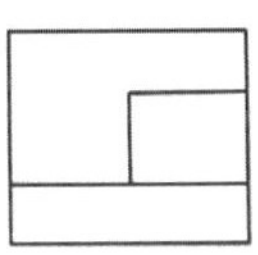 b. 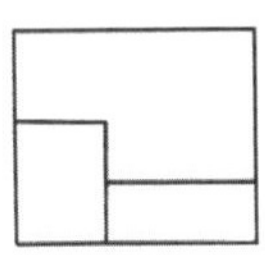 c. 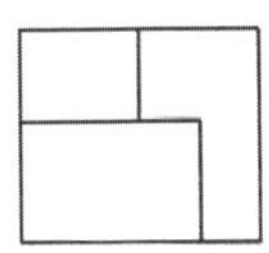 d. 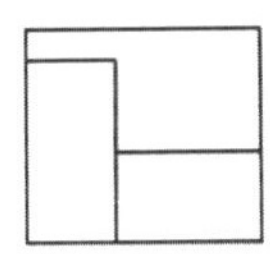

18. Which objects were cut out of a triangle to form this image?

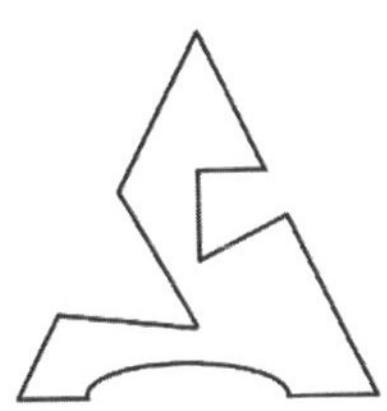

a.  b.  c. 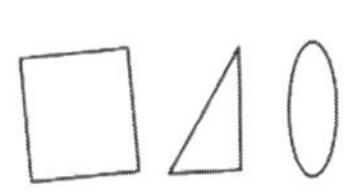 d. 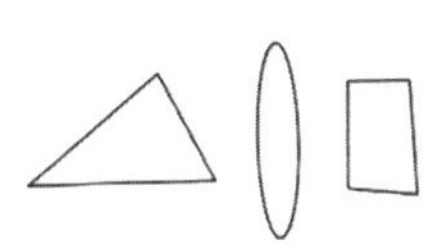

19. Which figure best represents what might result if the shapes shown on the left are cut out of the shape on the right?

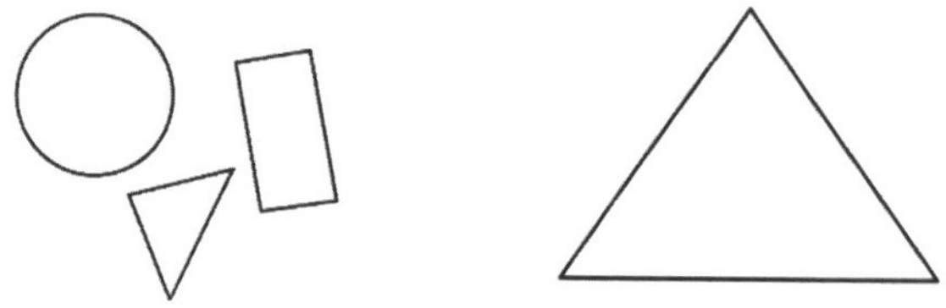

a. 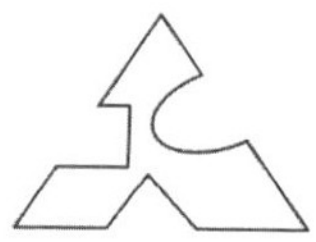 b. 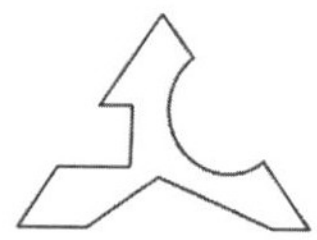 c. 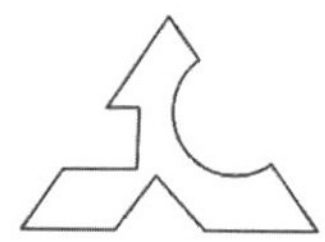 d. 

20. Which of the following configurations represents how the following objects might appear if they are rearranged?

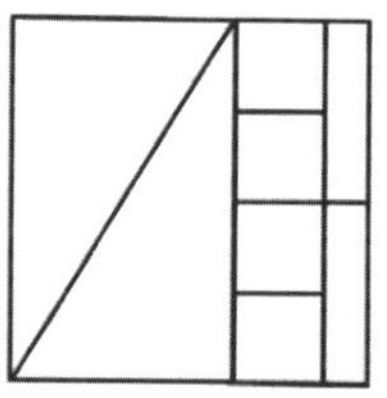

a. 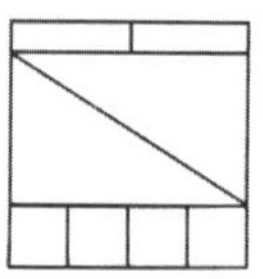 b. 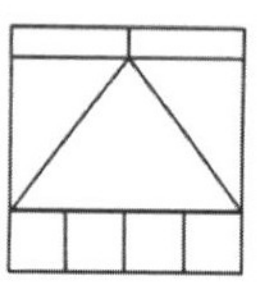 c. 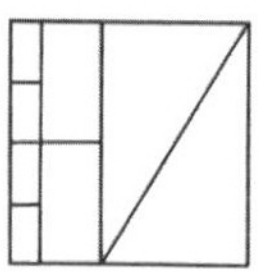 d. 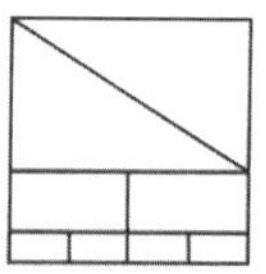

Mechanical Concepts

This is a test of your ability to understand mechanical concepts. Each question has a picture, a question and three possible answers. Read each question carefully, study the picture, and decide which answer is correct.

1. Two identical boxes are on inclines supported by identical springs. Which spring (A or B) will be more compressed? (If equal, mark C)

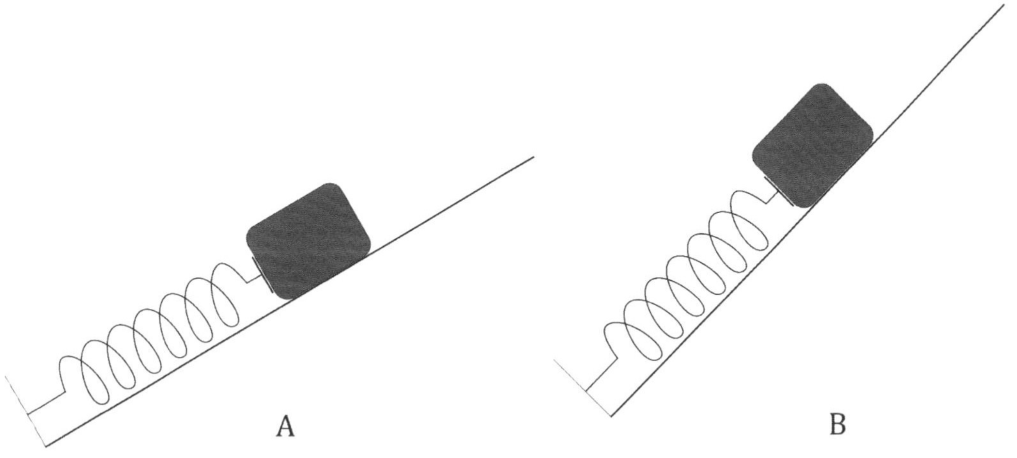

2. Two identical weights are held by a rope over a pulley. On one side of the rope, a second pulley is introduced. When the weights are released, will the left weight go up or down? (If the weight won't move, mark C)

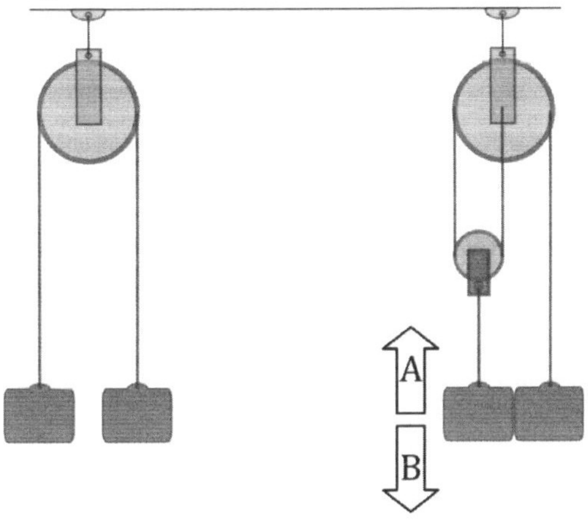

3. **The first of three touching rollers is rotating clockwise. What direction is the final roller spinning? (If the roller will not spin, mark C)**

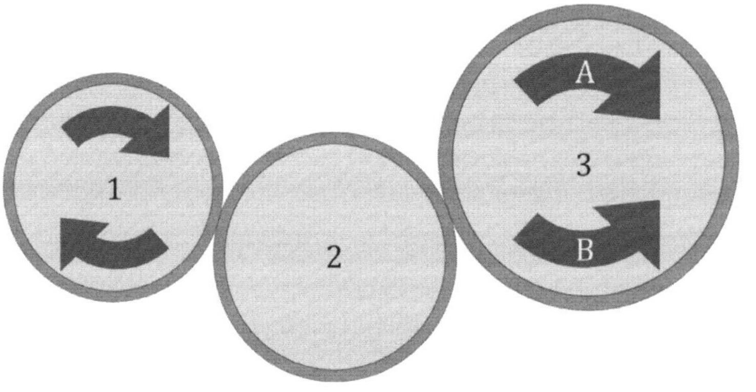

4. **A light car and a heavy truck drive towards each other at the same speed. When they crash, will they travel towards the left (A), travel towards the right (B), or not move at all (C)?**

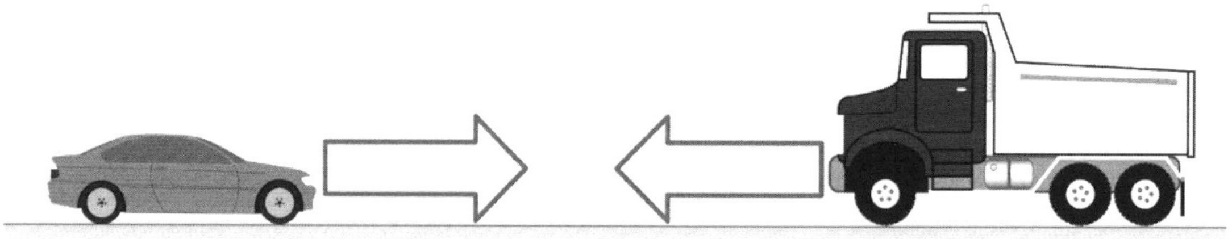

5. **Two identical funnels are placed in front of a fan. Which funnel will provide the greatest air speed at its exit? (If equal, mark C)**

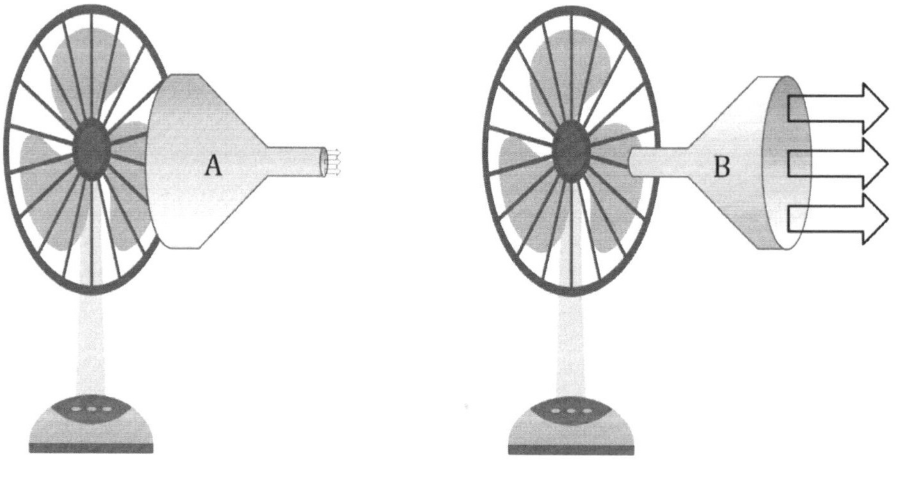

6. Two identical bricks are pushed, one over ice and one over dirt. Will the brick on ice require more force to push (A), less force to push (B), or the same force to push (C)?

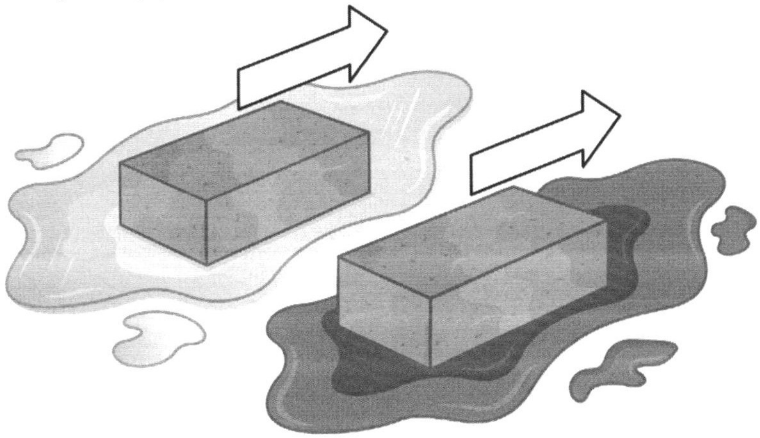

7. A plunger is pressed down a closed tube. Will the pressure inside increase (A), decrease (B), or stay the same (C)?

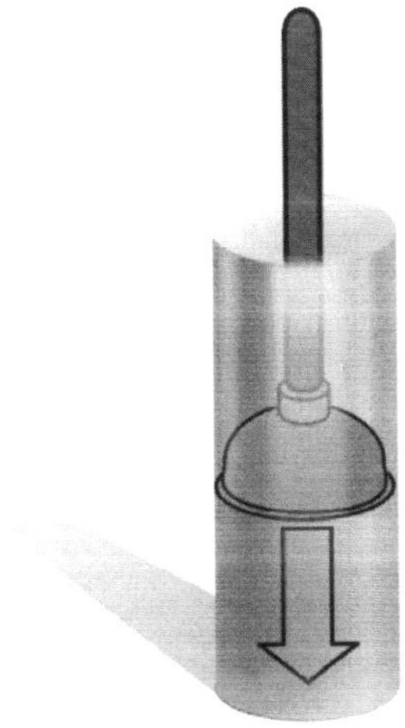

8. In this gear train, which gear is rotating with the highest number of revolutions per minute?

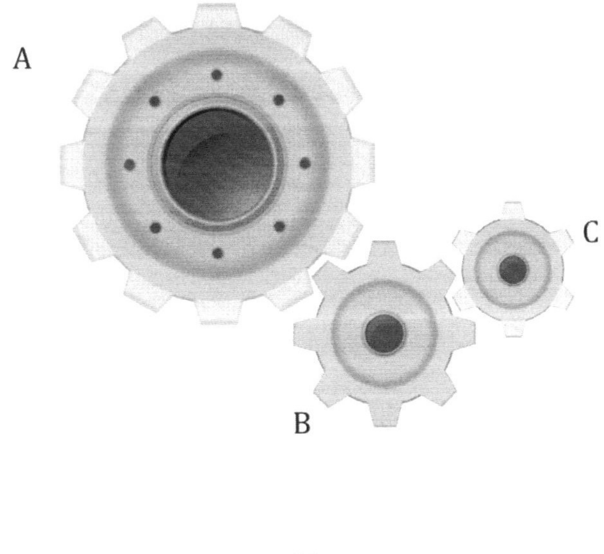

9. Which part of this box should be pushed to tip the box with the least amount of force?

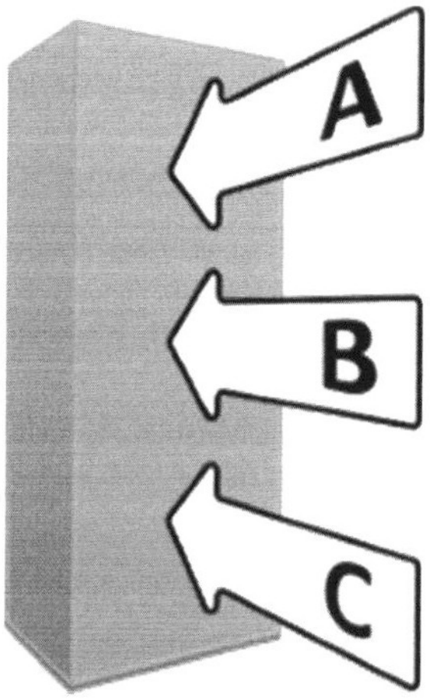

10. A boy throws a javelin off a cliff. In which part of the flight will the javelin have the greatest speed?

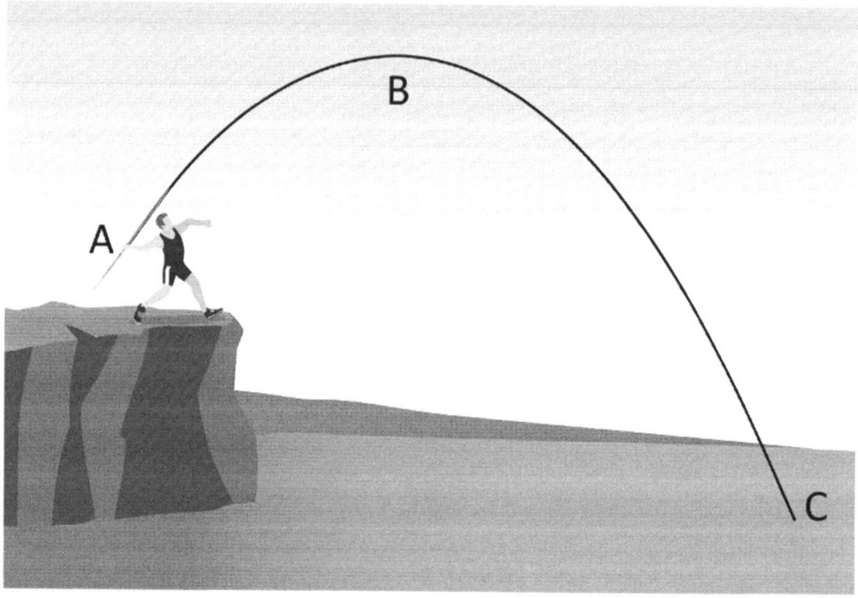

11. A 10-lb weight is placed on one side of a see-saw. A 5-lb weight is placed on the other side. Where does the center of the see-saw likely need to be located to balance the see-saw?

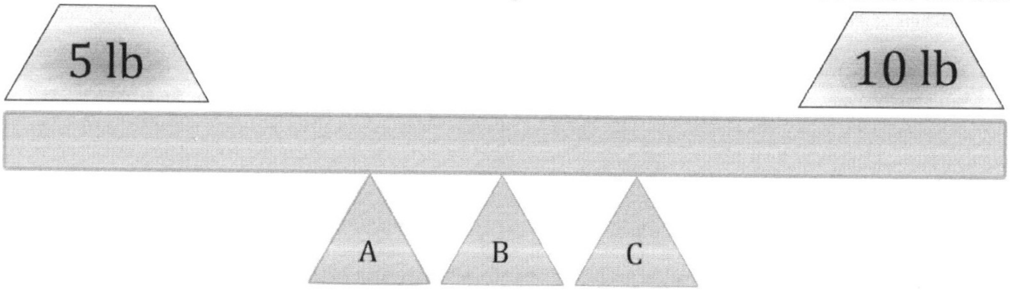

12. If the switch in this circuit is switched off, which light will turn off?

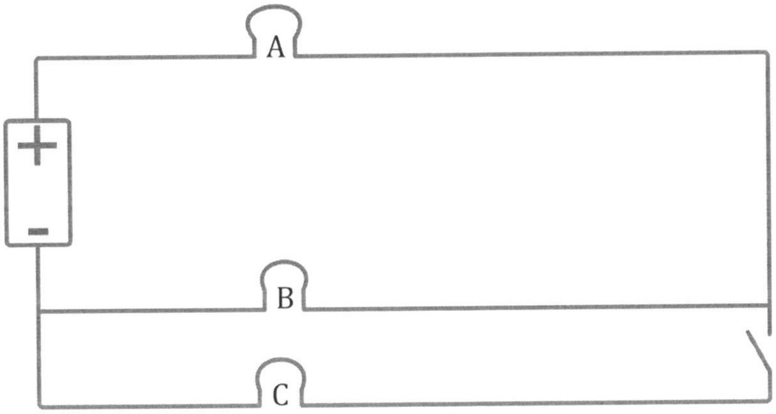

13. Most of the weight of a desk is in its drawers. If a strong person and a weak person want to lift the desk together, which side should the strong person lift? (If it makes no difference, mark C)

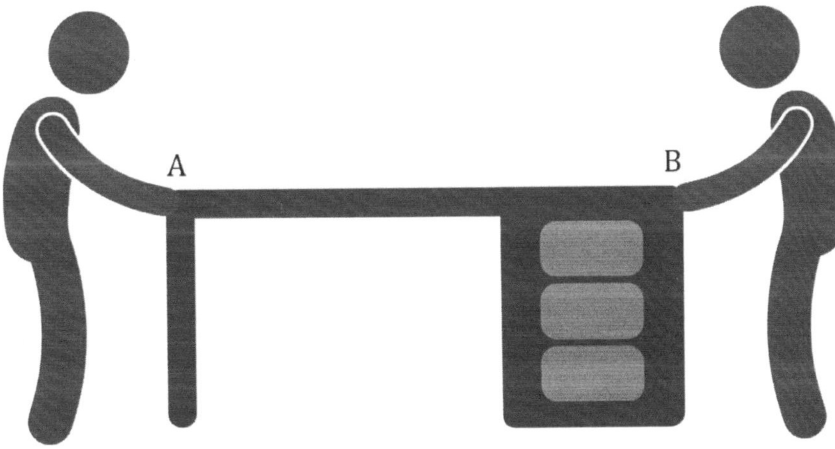

14. A motorcycle can drive its wheels at a maximum rotational speed. To go faster, should the driver replace the wheels with larger wheels or smaller wheels? (If equal, mark C)

15. **Will a boat ride higher in the water when it is floating in a swamp (A) or in a fresh-water river (B)? (If equal, mark C)**

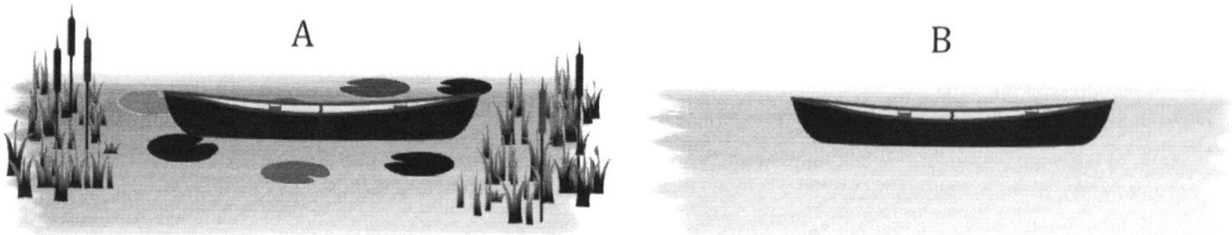

16. **Which opening in the dam will have the greatest water pressure?**

17. **Two wells are in the same environment. One has a wider opening than the other. If the air suddenly becomes very hot, which well will warm up more quickly? (If equal, mark C)**

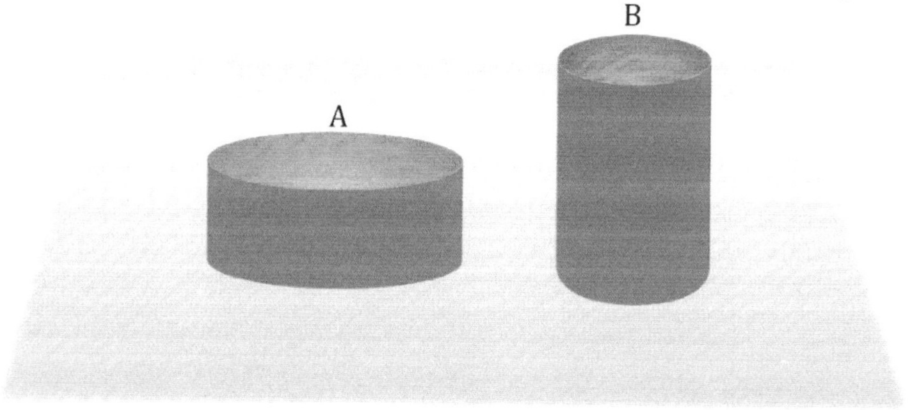

18. The amount of water is measured by a water height gauge on one side of a water tank. If the tank is installed on the shown slope, what point will the gauge read?

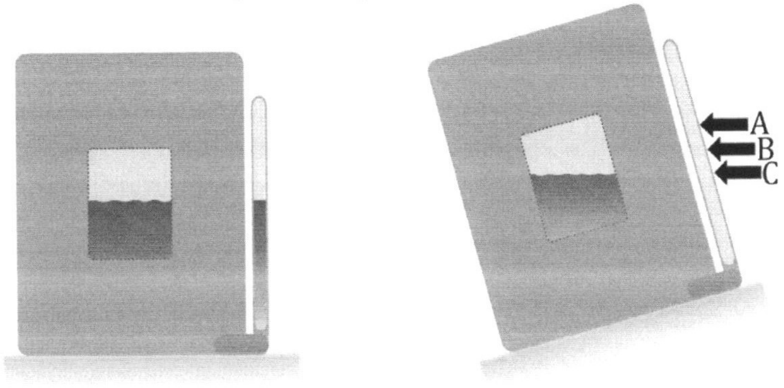

19. Two trucks are carrying the same weights. Which truck is more likely to tip during a turn? (If equal, mark C)

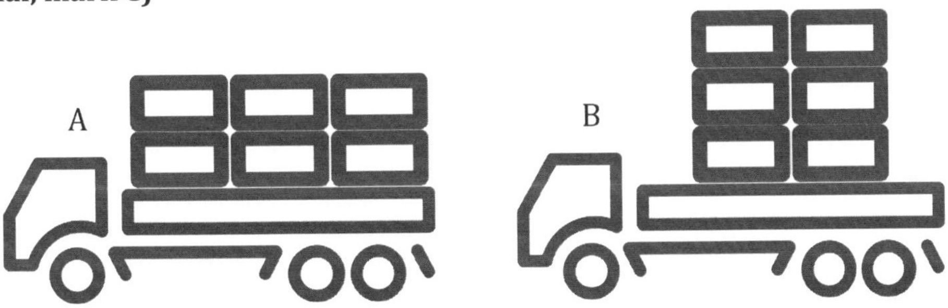

20. Which teapot design will hold the least amount of water? (If equal, mark C)

21. Two identical balls are pushed horizontally into identical springs. After the balls are released, which ball will go farther before stopping? (If equal, mark C)

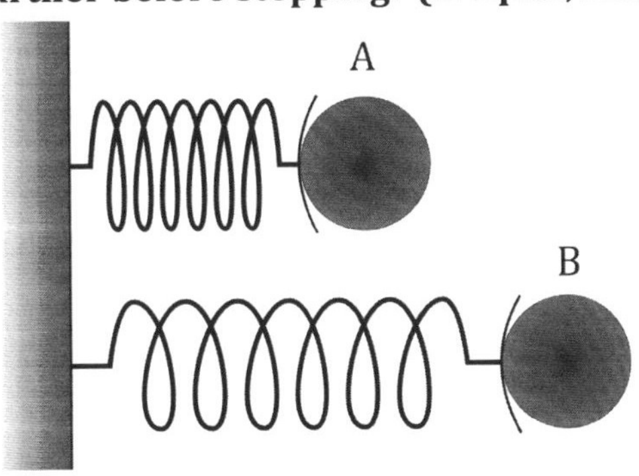

22. **Two flies are on a turntable. If the air around the turntable is still, which fly will feel the greatest breeze? (If equal, mark C)**

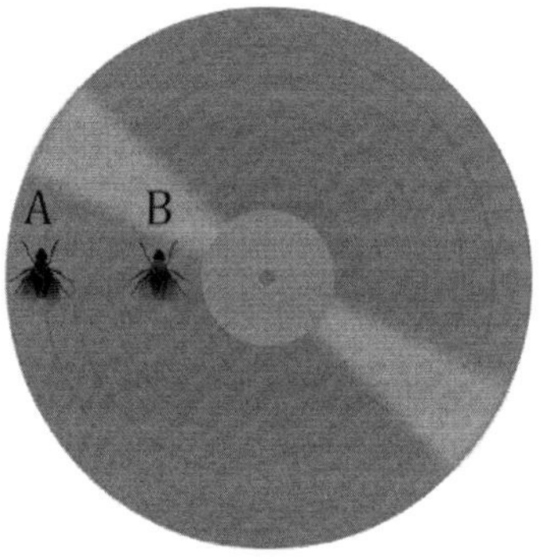

23. **Two bathtubs are completely full of water. Two solid rocks are placed in the bathtubs. Which bathtub will spill more water? (If equal, mark C)**

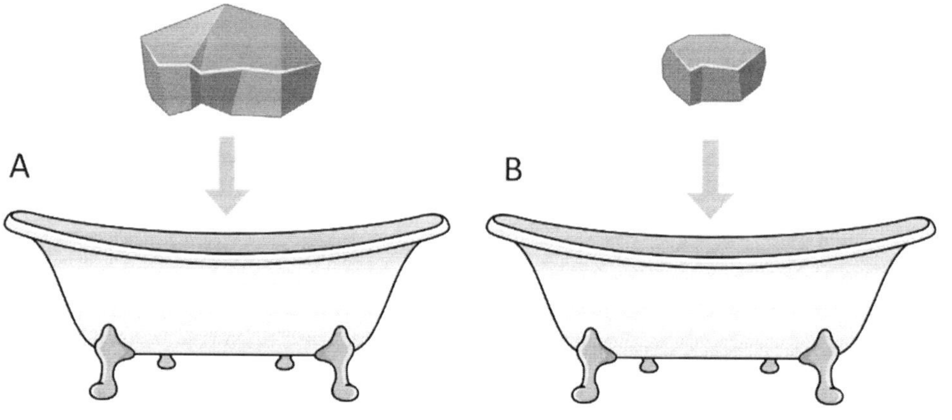

24. **A ball bounces off a hard, smooth wall. Assuming ideal conditions, where will the ball tend to go?**

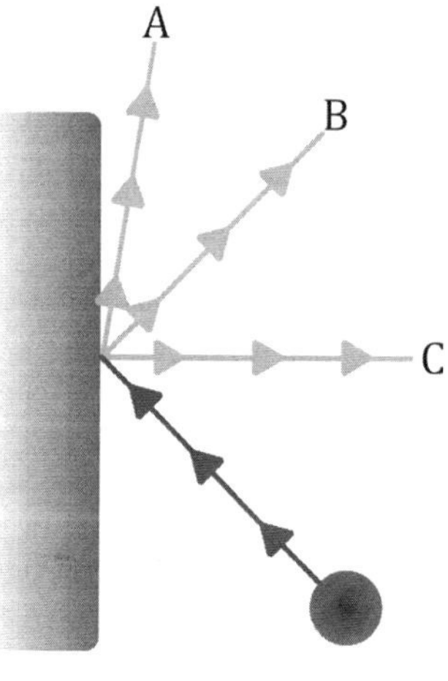

25. A spring is pointed up a rough hill. A ball is pushed into the spring. After the ball is released, it travels to point B. After the ball returns to the spring and bounces back up the hill, which point is it likely to reach?

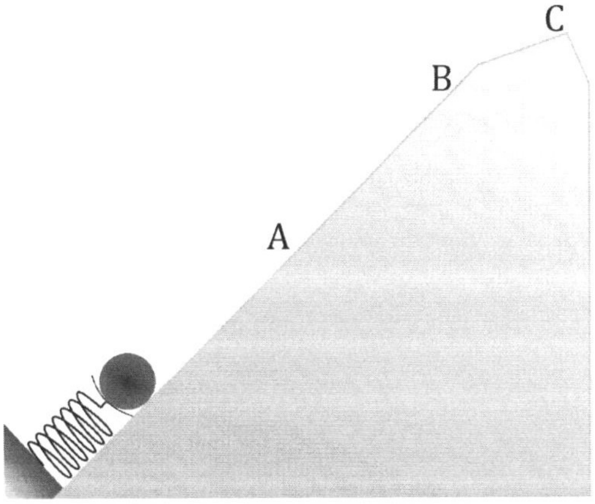

26. A sack of concrete is on a board. To tilt the board with the least amount of force, where should the man lift the board?

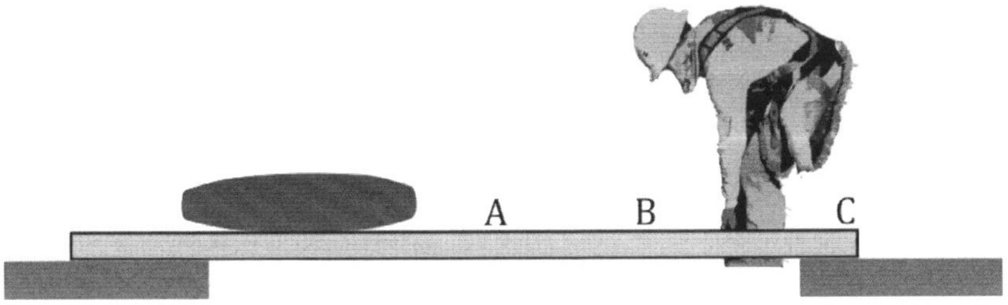

27. A bowling ball and a tennis ball are dropped from the same height onto identical springs. Which spring will compress more? (If equal, mark C)

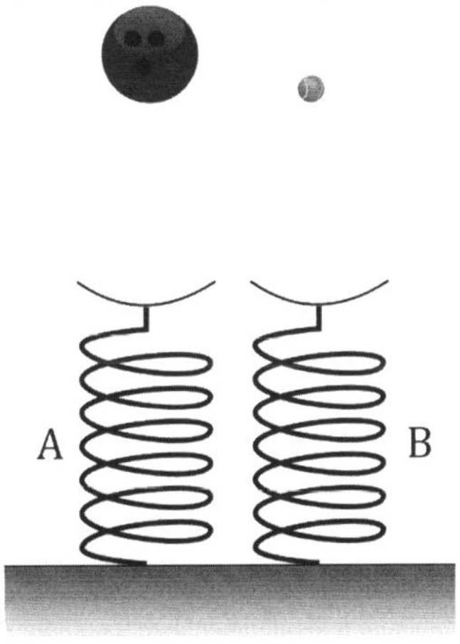

28. Two identical motors pull ropes with the same constant speed off spools. Which spool will have the greater rotational speed? (If equal, mark C)

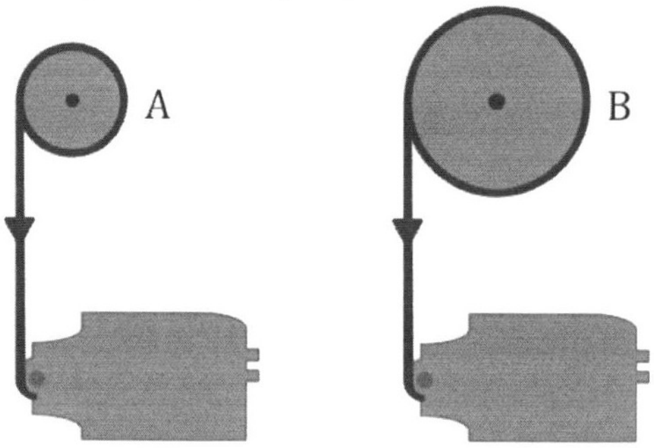

29. A pipe is cut in two to install a viewing port to see the water. Where will the water travel slowest?

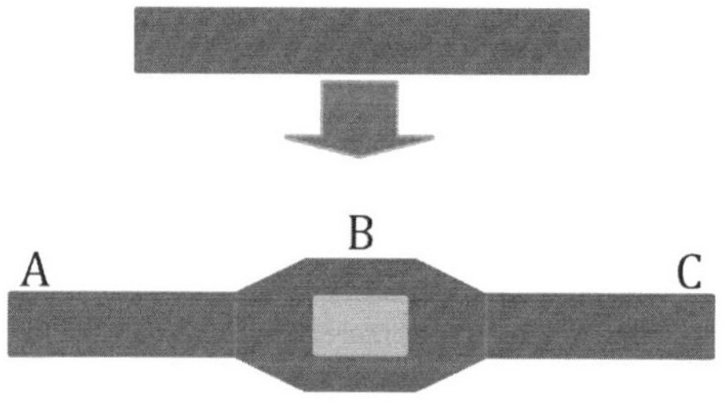

30. A heavy sack of sand falls off a building at the same time that a water bottle falls off the same building. Assuming negligible air resistance, will the sack of sand land before (A), after (B), or at the same time (C) as the water bottle?

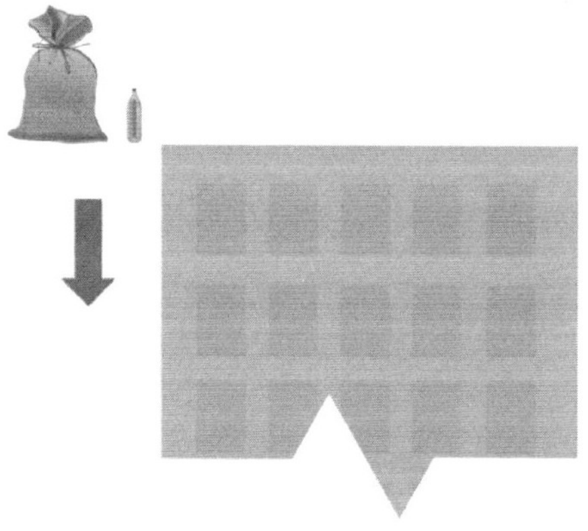

31. A child is swinging on the outside of a merry-go-round. If the child lets go of the merry-go-round, before he touches the ground, what direction will he tend to go?

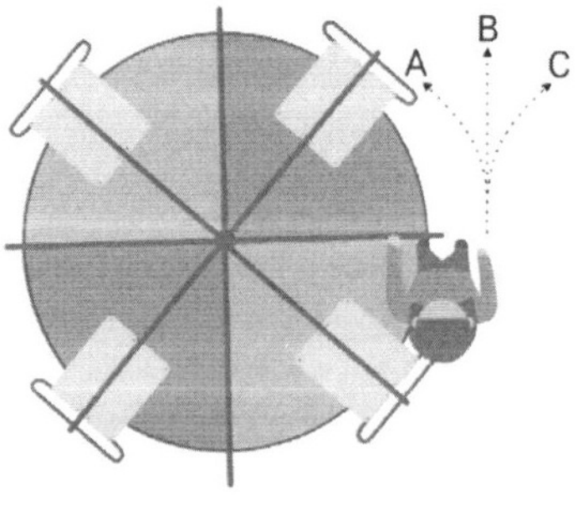

32. A measuring wheel measures distance by rolling a wheel on the ground and counting the number of rotations of that wheel. If someone replaces the wheel with a larger wheel, will the measuring device measure distances to be longer (A), shorter (B), or the same distance (C) as they actually are?

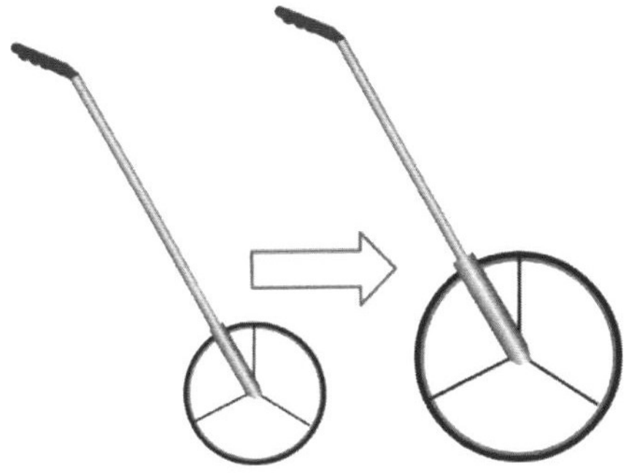

33. A cup of coffee is set in a cup holder in a car. If the car curves left around a corner too quickly, which direction will the coffee spill?

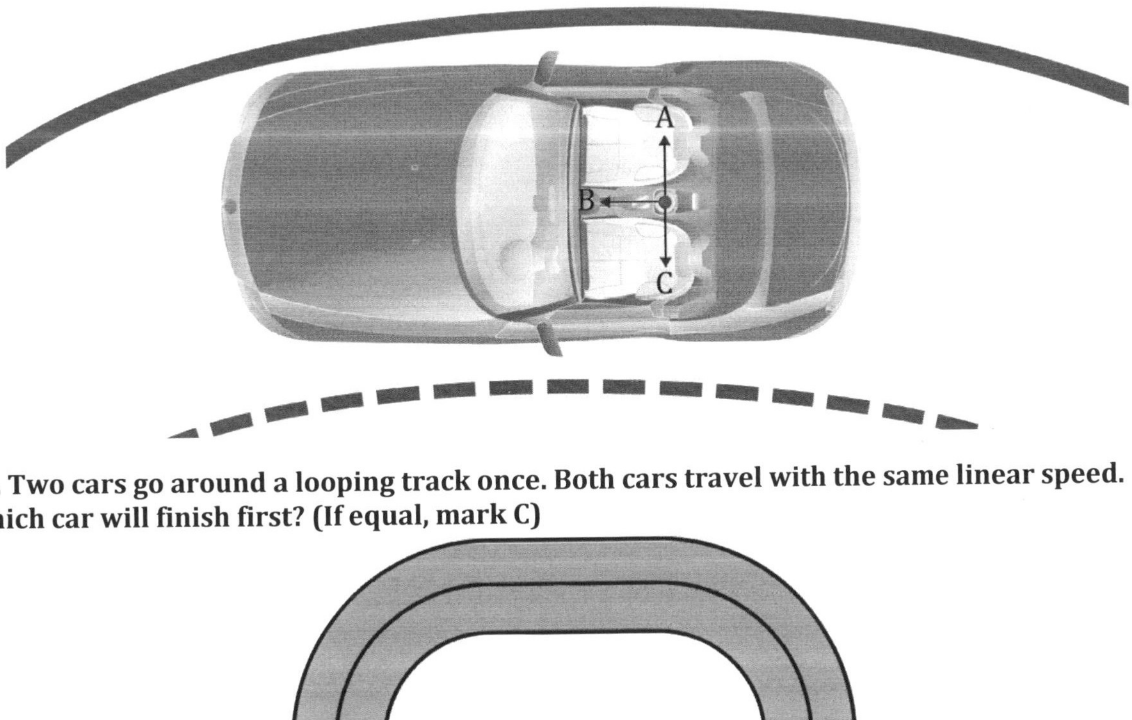

34. Two cars go around a looping track once. Both cars travel with the same linear speed. Which car will finish first? (If equal, mark C)

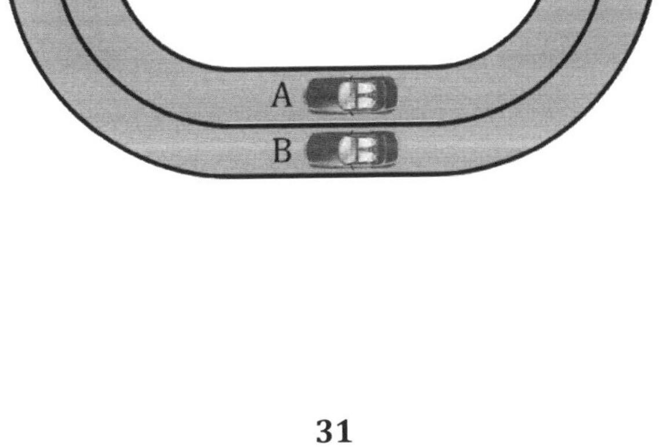

35. Which ramp will make it easiest to roll the cart up into the truck? (If equal, mark C)

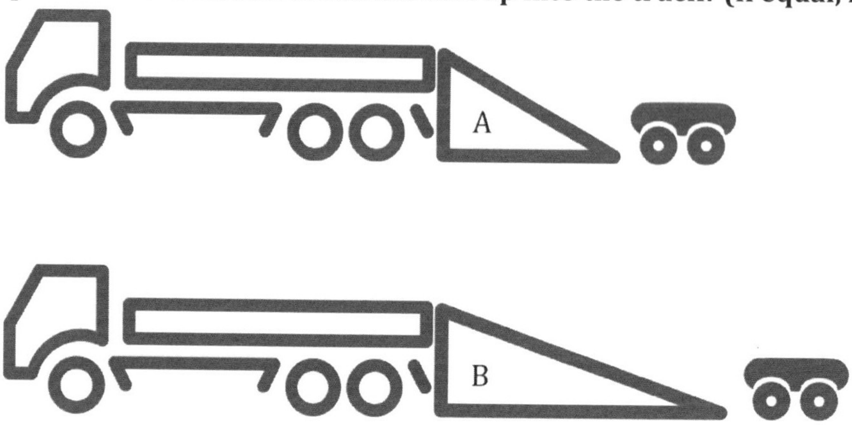

36. A drifting sailboat collides with a drifting small dinghy. Which direction will the sailboat tend to go?

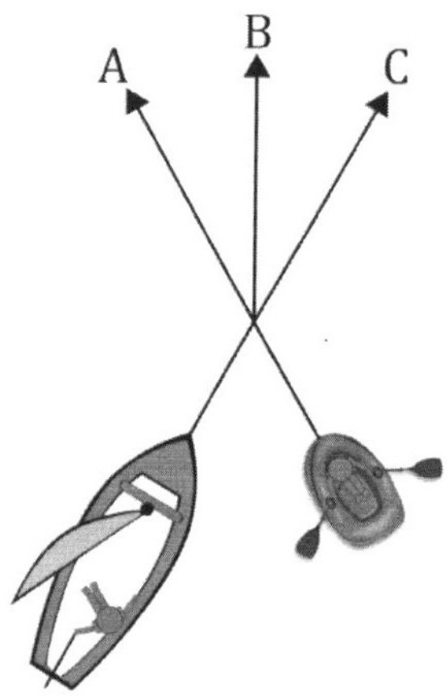

37. A pair of identical gears is run by one large central gear. Which gear spins faster? (If equal, mark C)

38. A large man and a small man are trying to use the see-saw. Where should the large man sit to balance the see-saw?

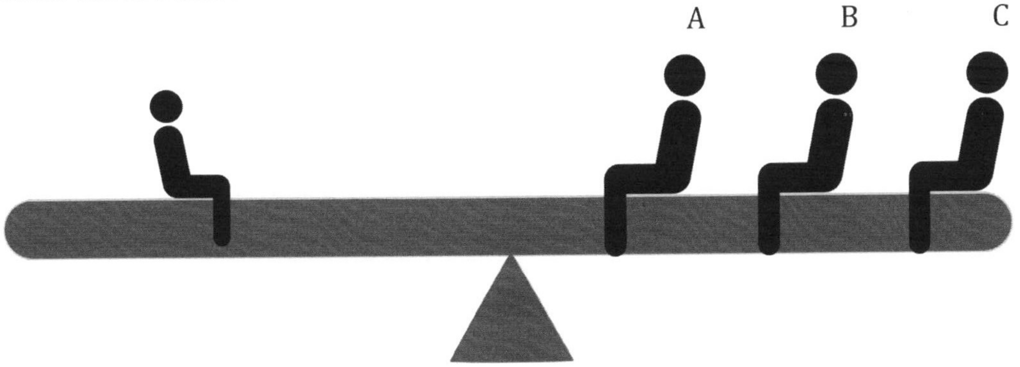

39. Two fans spin at the same rotational speed. One fan has longer blades. Which fan will move more air? (If equal, mark C)

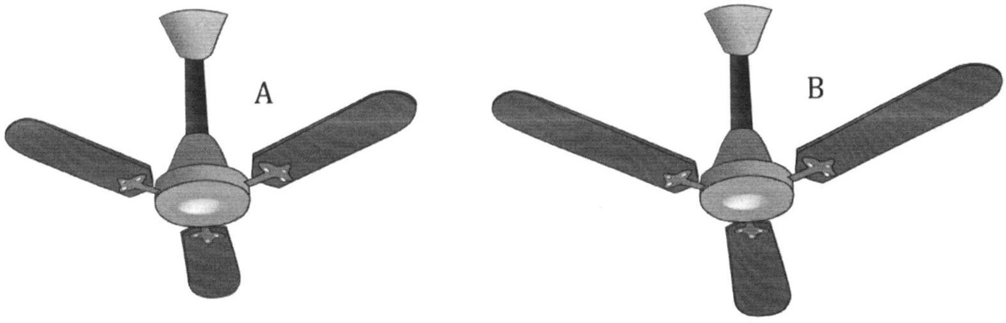

40. An above ground swimming pool has a patch on one side near the base. Which height of water is most likely to break the patch? (If equal, mark C)

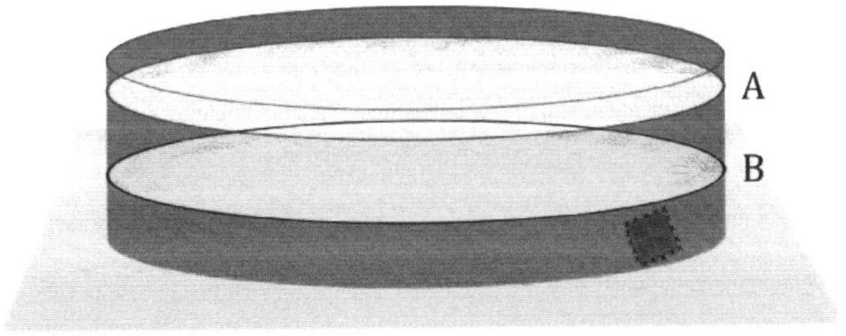

41. Two identical springs are pointed up a hill. Identical balls are pushed into the springs to different locations. Which ball will go higher up the hill before returning? (If equal, mark C)

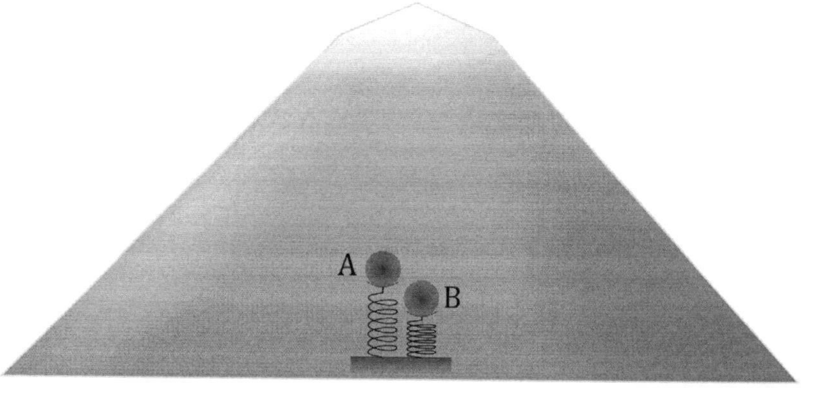

42. A man stands near the edge of a wooden bridge over a stream. Which set of bridge supports holds the most amount of weight? (If equal, mark C)

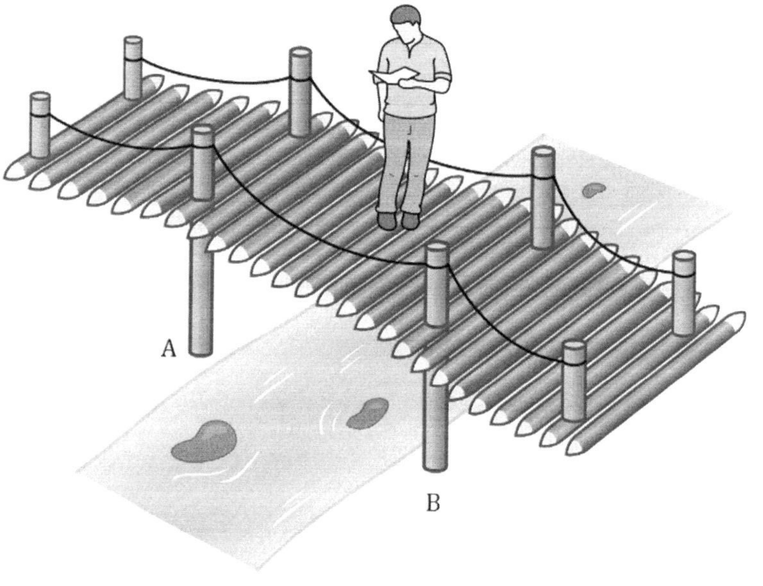

43. Two weights, one forty-pound weight and one eighty-pound weight, are dropped from a height of four feet over the ground. Which weight will hit the ground first? (If equal, mark C)

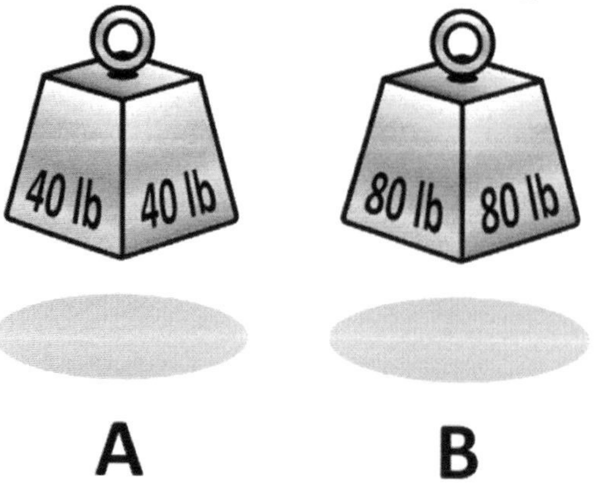

44. A fly is holding onto a Frisbee which is spinning through the air. Will the fly be able to hold on easier at the edge or in the center of the Frisbee? (If equal, mark C)

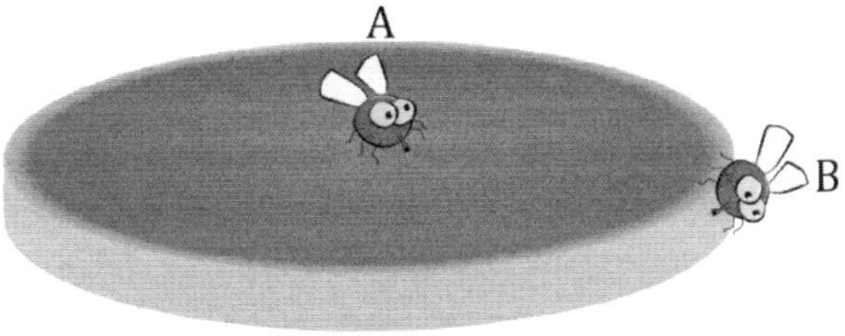

Answers and Explanations

Mathematical Usage

1. A:

$$1\text{ quart } \times \frac{1\text{ gallons}}{4\text{ quarts}} = 0.25\text{ gallons}$$

2. C:

$$60\text{ rods} \times \frac{1\text{ furlong}}{40\text{ rods}} = 1.5\text{ furlongs}$$

3. D:

$$2\text{ slugs} \times \frac{14.59\text{ kilograms}}{1\text{ slug}} \times \frac{1{,}000\text{ grams}}{1\text{ kilogram}} = 29{,}180\text{ grams}$$

4. C:

$$87{,}120\text{ sq ft} \times \frac{1\text{ acre}}{43{,}560\text{ sq ft}} = 2\text{ acres}$$

5. D:

$$4\text{ miles} \times \frac{1.609\text{ kilometers}}{1\text{ mile}} = 6.436\text{ kilometers}$$

6. B:

$$0.5\text{ pounds } \times \frac{16\text{ ounces}}{1\text{ pounds}} = 8\text{ ounces}$$

7. A:

$$12\text{ feet} \times \frac{1\text{ fathom}}{6\text{ feet}} = 2\text{ fathoms}$$

8. C:

$$2\text{ barrels} \times \frac{42\text{ gallons}}{1\text{ barrel}} = 84\text{ gallons}$$

9. C:

$$4\text{ kilograms} \times \frac{2.2\text{ pounds}}{1\text{ kilogram}} = 8.8\text{ pounds}$$

10. D:

$$5 \text{ kilograms} \times \frac{1{,}000 \text{ grams}}{1 \text{ kilogram}} = 5{,}000 \text{ grams}$$

11. D:

$$5 \text{ hands} \times \frac{10 \text{ centimeters}}{1 \text{ hand}} = 50 \text{ centimeters}$$

12. C:

$$17.6 \text{ feet/second} \times \frac{3 \text{ miles/hour}}{4.4 \text{ feet/second}} = 12 \text{ miles/hour}$$

13. B:

$$1 \text{ barrel} \times \frac{42 \text{ gallons}}{1 \text{ barrel}} \times \frac{4 \text{ quarts}}{1 \text{ gallon}} = 168 \text{ quarts}$$

14. A:

$$5{,}280 \text{ inches} \times \frac{1 \text{ foot}}{12 \text{ inches}} \times \frac{1 \text{ mile}}{5{,}280 \text{ feet}} = \frac{1}{12} \text{ miles}$$

15. B:

$$2 \text{ feet} \times \frac{12 \text{ inches}}{1 \text{ foot}} \times \frac{2.54 \text{ centimeters}}{1 \text{ inch}} \times \frac{1 \text{ hand}}{10 \text{ centimeters}} = 6.096 \text{ hands}$$

16. E:

$$7 \text{ pints} \times \frac{1 \text{ quart}}{2 \text{ pints}} \times \frac{1 \text{ gallon}}{4 \text{ quarts}} = \frac{7}{8} \text{ gallons} = 0.875 \text{ gallons}$$

17. C:

$$16 \text{ quarts} \times \frac{1 \text{ gallon}}{4 \text{ quarts}} \times \frac{3.785 \text{ liters}}{1 \text{ gallon}} = 15.14 \text{ liters}$$

18. C:

$$4 \text{ feet} \times \frac{12 \text{ inches}}{1 \text{ foot}} \times \frac{2.54 \text{ centimeters}}{1 \text{ inch}} = 121.92 \text{ centimeters}$$

Reading for Comprehension

1. A: In the first sentence of the third paragraph, it states that decaying marine organisms are the source of oil and natural gas.

2. C: This subject is introduced in the first sentence: "Oil and natural gas are the products of decaying marine organisms." The rest of the paragraph elaborates this subject.

3. B: The second-to-last sentence of the passage states that the raw oil pumped to the surface of an oil well is called petroleum.

4. D: The final paragraph describes how oil companies will drill exploratory wells at a prospective site before bringing in the permanent equipment. This suggests that the exploratory wells are less expensive.

5. A: This is explicit in the third sentence of the second paragraph: "Between 250 and 300 million years ago, large swaths of the eastern United States were swampy, which explains the rich coal deposits that are found there today."

6. B: The passage is devoted to answering this question. It addresses the material sources of fossil fuels, as well as the geographic and geological locations of the best sources.

7. B: This is explained in the second and third sentences of the last paragraph, particularly in the third, where it says that, "Unless there is a border of nonporous rock, the oil and natural gas will be distributed over a much larger area, which will make it more difficult to access."

8. D: This is mentioned throughout the passage, but it is stated explicitly in the first sentence of the fourth paragraph.

9. D: The fourth sentence of the second paragraph describes how the absorption of extra neutrons converts U^{238} into plutonium.

10. A: The second sentence of the passage suggests that the desire for new nuclear plants has waned since the 1960s. This point is further developed in the first sentence of the fourth paragraph, which states that "the demand for new nuclear reactors has declined, and the concern over limited supplies of uranium has diminished."

11. B: The third sentence of the fourth paragraph states that France, Russia, and Japan are the countries that use breeder reactors for commercial purposes.

12. C: This information is in the fourth sentence of the third paragraph.

13. C: The second sentence of the third paragraph states, "The plutonium used in a breeder reactor has a much longer half-life than U^{235}, so a meltdown would be much more catastrophic."

14. A: Fast breeder reactors are discussed in the third paragraph. The third sentence of this paragraph states that this reactor uses "'fast' neutrons, which must be slowed down with a neutron moderator so that they can sustain a chain reaction."

15. D: The third sentence of the third paragraph states that, "In a gas turbine power plant, the bulk of the fuel consumption goes toward powering the compressor, and a great deal of heat is lost through the exhaust gases." The other answer choices are all real advantages of the gas turbine power plant and are described in the second paragraph.

16. A: Intercoolers are described in the fourth sentence of the last paragraph.

17. B: The third paragraph of the passage deals primarily with the disadvantages of gas turbine power plants, as indicated by the introductory sentence: "There are, however, some drawbacks to the gas turbine power plant."

18. D: This comparison is made in the third sentence, which states that "The gas turbine power plant is similar to a steam power plant." The similarity of operation is then described in the next couple of sentences.

19. A: A regenerator heats up compressed air before it enters the combustion chamber. This is mentioned in the third sentence of the final paragraph.

20. B: This is implied throughout the article, but it is explicit in the second sentence of the third paragraph: "The major disadvantage of these plants is that they produce little net output relative to their consumption of fuel."

21. C: The passage describes the various methods of converting primary energy sources into electricity.

22. A: The second sentence of the third paragraph states that simple generators "lose energy through heat and whatever friction exists in the workings of the machine." Therefore, it would seem likely that lubricating the parts of the generator would improve the efficiency.

23. A: The first sentence of this paragraph introduces this idea: "These simple generators create a great deal of waste." The paragraph goes on to describe the ways in which energy is lost and then concludes by stating that "it takes three units of primary energy to create one unit of electricity."

24. B: This information is given in the last sentence of the first paragraph.

25. D: The first sentence of the fourth paragraph states that turbogenerators are more powerful than simple generators.

26. B: The final sentence of the fourth paragraph states that "the most common primary energy sources for turbogenerators are coal, oil, and nuclear power."

27. D: The first sentence of the fourth paragraph states that the turbogenerator is "so named because it combines a turbine with a generator."

28. A: This can be inferred from the last sentence of the passage: "There is also an ongoing effort to develop wind turbines that can efficiently produce large amounts of power." Clearly, these turbines have not yet been made efficient.

29. B: The passage begins by discussing the diminished demand for nuclear power plants in the past couple of decades. It then goes on to discuss how one of the reasons for this is the rising cost.

30. B: This information is given in the second sentence of the fourth paragraph.

31. C: The final sentence of the third paragraph states that "the United States government has been less willing to subsidize an unpopular industry."

32. A: The first sentence of the fourth paragraph refers to the "shorter-than-expected" lifespan of nuclear power plants. The remainder of the paragraph describes the reasons for this phenomenon.

33. D: Embrittlement is degradation of the reactor vessel by continuous neutron bombardment. This is stated in the last sentence of the fourth paragraph.

34. D: These consequences are described in the second and third paragraphs.

35. A: At the end of the first paragraph, it states that in the 1960s and 70s, "more new [nuclear] power plants were built than were needed." The passages then states that "This has diminished demand for every type of power plant."

36. D: In the last sentence of the passage, it states that the owners of decommissioned nuclear power plants often spend a great deal of time and money trying to dispose of material and equipment.

Assembling Objects

Question	Answer
1.	C
2.	C
3.	B
4.	D
5.	A
6.	C
7.	A
8.	B
9.	B
10.	B
11.	D
12.	D
13.	D
14.	D
15.	C
16.	A
17.	B
18.	A
19.	C
20.	A

Mechanical Concepts

1. B: The object on spring B will exert more force into its spring than the object on spring A because more of the weight will be supported by the spring rather than the incline. Spring B will compress more under the larger force.

2. A: In the rope in the pulleys, forces are constant. The weight on the left is supported by two sections of the rope. Two sections of the rope pull with more force than one section of the rope. Therefore, the left weight will go up (A) and the right weight will go down.

3. A: In rollers, adjacent rollers spin in opposite directions. Thus, roller 2 spins counter-clockwise, and roller 3 spins in a clockwise direction.

4. A: Because the truck is heavier, the car will not be able to stop the truck. Thus, they will move to the left because of the imbalanced force.

5. A: The amount of air entering the funnel must be the same as the amount of air exiting the funnel. The air in funnel A has to exit faster to allow for the greater amount of moving air.

6. B: The friction acting on the brick on ice will be less than the friction on the other brick. Thus, the brick on ice will require less force to push.

7. A: Decreasing the volume of space for a set amount of gas increases the pressure inside.

8. C: When two cogs mesh, the cog with fewer teeth spins faster. Thus, cog B spins faster than cog A. Cog C spins faster than cog B.

9. A: Pushing at A provides a greater moment around the tipping point which allows for the least amount of force required.

10. C: Since air resistance on a javelin is negligible, and its horizontal velocity is effectively constant throughout its flight, the fastest point will be the point that has the greatest vertical velocity. Since point C is the lowest point, it is the point at which the maximum potential energy will have been converted to kinetic energy.

11. C: Because the weight on the right is twice the weight of the left, the center (fulcrum) of the see-saw needs to be closer to the right side.

12. C: Disconnecting the switch will stop the flow of electricity through light C which is required for the light to be on.

13. B: The strong man should be closest to the most weight which is on the side of the drawers.

14. A: If rotational speed is the same, large wheels have a greater linear velocity on the outside than small wheels.

15. C: Because the density of water is essentially the same in both situations, the boat will float equally high in both locations.

16. C: Water pressure increases with depth. Opening C is at the greatest depth of water, which means it is the point with the greatest amount of pressure.

17. A: Well A will be more affected by the air temperature because it has a larger surface area exposed to the air.

18. C: The water level will stay constant across all open tubes. Placing the tank on the slope will lower the water in the gauge.

19. B: The center of gravity in truck B is higher, making it easier to tip.

20. B: The water in teapot A will overflow only when the water reaches the level of the lid. However, the water in teapot B will overflow when the water level is at the top of the spout.

21. A: Because potential energy increases with the amount of compression, ball A will have more energy to convert to kinetic energy.

22. A: Because the linear velocity increases with radius, fly A will travel at a greater speed and thus feel the greatest breeze.

23. A: The larger rock has a greater volume than the smaller rock and will displace an equivalently greater amount of water.

24. B: The ball will bounce off the wall at an angle (angle of reflection) identical to the angle with which it hit the wall (angle of incidence) relative to the normal line at the point of impact.

25. A: Due to frictional losses, the ball is not likely to return to the same height on the second trip.

26. C: The force to lift the board decreases as the distance from the concrete increases.

27. A: Because the bowling ball weighs more than the tennis ball, it has a greater potential energy. This energy will cause the bowling ball's spring to compress more than the tennis ball's spring.

28. A: The ropes will pull at a certain constant linear speed. But, the lower radius of spool A will make for a greater rotational speed and revolution count.

29. B: Because the same amount of water has to flow through all sections of the pipe, the portion with the largest cross-sectional area will need to have a lower velocity.

30. C: Assuming negligible air resistance, the acceleration of an object in freefall is independent of the object's size, shape, or mass. Thus, both objects will fall at the same rate and land at the same time.

31. B: Once the child lets go of the merry-go-round, he is not under any external forces and will continue traveling in a straight line tangential to the circular path.

32. B: The larger wheel will not rotate as much as the smaller wheel going the same distance. Because the device only measures rotation, the device will measure distances to be shorter than they actually are.

33. A: The coffee cup will be accelerating inward with the car, but the fluid inside the cup has no external force acting upon it and wants to continue in the same path it was going before due to inertia. In relation to the direction the car is going, the coffee will spill toward A. If the car slammed on the brakes instead of turning, it would spill in the direction of B.

34. A: The car on the inside travels less distance to complete a loop. Because the cars have the same speed, car A will travel its shorter distance faster than car B can travel its longer distance.

35. B: The longer ramp has a less steep slope, or greater mechanical advantage, and requires less force to ascend.

36. C: Because the sailboat is large relative to the dinghy, the sailboat will continue with its course unhindered due to the imbalanced force.

37. C: Because the outer gears have the same number of teeth and are driven by the same gear, they will spin at the same rate.

38. A: Because the force of the large man exerts a larger torque on the see-saw than the small man at the same radius, the large man should be closer to the center of the see-saw than the small man.

39. B: The fan with the longer blades has more surface area to contact and push more air per rotation.

40. A: The patch will break with the highest pressure. The pressure at the patch will increase if there is a higher water level.

41. B: Potential energy increases with the amount of compression; thus, ball B will go higher up the hill after it is released.

42. B: More of the man's weight is on the set of supports closest to him.

43. C: Assuming negligible air resistance, the acceleration of an object in freefall is independent of the object's size, shape, or mass. Since both objects are of significant mass and their fall is of such brief duration that no significant air resistance will be generated, both objects will fall at the same rate and land at the same time.

44. A: The absolute velocity of the flies depends on their distance from the center of the Frisbee. Fly B will be traveling much faster than fly A, thus experiencing more air resistance and significantly greater difficulty hanging onto the frisbee.

Practice Test #2

Mathematical Usage

Use the following information to answer questions 1-18:

1 acre	=	43,560 square feet
1 barrel	=	42 gallons
1 fathom	=	6 feet
1 foot	=	12 inches
1 furlong	=	40 rods
1 gallon	=	3.785 liters
1 gallon	=	4 quarts
1 hand	=	10 centimeters
1 inch	=	2.54 centimeters
1 kilogram	=	1,000 grams
1 kilogram	=	2.2 pounds
1 kilometer	=	1,000 meters
1 mile	=	1.609 kilometers
1 mile	=	5,280 feet
3 mile/hour	=	4.4 feet/second
1 pint	=	4 gills
1 pound	=	16 ounces
1 quart	=	2 pints
1 slug	=	14.59 kilograms
1 square mile	=	640 acres

If none of the answers listed are correct, select answer e, N for none of the above.

1. 420 gallons = ? barrels

a. 1
b. 2.43
c. 5
d. 10
e. N

2. $\frac{1}{16}$ kilogram = ? ounces

a. 1.4
b. 2.2
c. 4.4
d. 8
e. N

3. 2.2 pounds = ? grams

a. 1,000
b. 1,200
c. 1,500
d. 2,200
e. N

4. 7.2 kilograms = ? slugs

a. 0.493
b. 72
c. 7132
d. 720
e. N

5. 2,450 centimeters = ? kilometers

a. 0.00245
b. 0.0245
c. 0.245
d. 2.45
e. N

6. 720 acres = ? square miles

a. 1.125
b. 1.85
c. 7.21
d. 250
e. N

7. 72 fathoms = ? feet

a. 2
b. 12
c. 72
d. 432
e. N

8. 7.2 pints = ? gallons

a. 0.75
b. 0.9
c. 1.2
d. 1.27
e. N

9. 8 quarts = ? liters

a. 2
b. 3.785
c. 7.57
d. 8
e. N

10. 0.035 grams = ? kilograms

a. 0.000035
b. 0.05
c. 35
d. 35,000
e. N

11. 9 miles/hour = ? feet/second

a. 12.3
b. 13.2
c. 23.1
d. 31.2
e. N

12. 15 kilograms = ? slugs. Round your answer to the nearest hundredth place.

a. 0.07
b. 0.97
c. 1.03
d. 5.22
e. N

13. 10,560 feet = ? kilometers

a. 1.609
b. 3.218
c. 4.827
d. 6.436
e. N

14. 3.785 liters = ? quarts

a. 0.946
b. 1.057
c. 3.875
d. 4
e. N

15. 1,500 grams = ? pounds

a. 1.1
b. 2.2
c. 3.3
d. 4.4
e. N

16. 25.4 hands = ? inches

a. 10
b. 20
c. 50
d. 100
e. N

17. 2 gallons = ? gills

a. 16
b. 32
c. 64
d. 128
e. N

18. 10 fathoms = ? inches

a. 7.2
b. 72
c. 120
d. 720
e. N

Reading for Comprehension

Passage #1

Materials may be classified as insulators or conductors, depending on the ease with which they allow the passage of charges. An insulator may have a charge generated in one area, without the charge being distributed throughout the rest of the object. Amber and rubber are two classic examples of insulators. A conductor, meanwhile, is a material through which a charge can move quite freely. Almost all metals are excellent conductors: two of the metals most commonly used as conductors in industry are copper and aluminum. Some gases, as for instance ionized plasma, are also useful conductors.

When a charge is generated within a conductor, it will almost immediately distribute itself evenly throughout the object. In part, this is because the charge will have a single polarity (i.e., either positive or negative), and so the components of the charge will repel one another. The reason why a conductor allows the movement of a charge is because the atoms of the material are able to detach an electron easily. These detached electrons can move freely about the object and will behave almost like gas molecules. By contrast, the atoms in an insulator will not allow their electrons to detach, and therefore, the charge will not distribute.

Many materials combine elements of insulators and conductors. One interesting case is the photoconductor, a material that is an insulator in the dark, but will conduct a charge when light shines upon it. The element selenium is one example of a photoconductor, which is why this material is used in photocopying machines. In a standard photocopying machine, the surface of a plate or cylinder is coated with selenium, which becomes electrically charged after it goes past a series of wires. The original document is then projected through a lens onto the surface. In the places where the image is dark, the charge is retained; in the areas that light can shine through, the charge is drained. A negatively charged toner or dry ink is then applied to the latent image, so that it may be seen. The positively charged paper attracts this dry ink from the plate, which forms a direct positive image. This image is then fused onto the surface of the paper with heat.

Some materials are neither pure insulators nor pure conductors. These materials, known as semiconductors, are often composites of several elements. By adjusting the relative amounts of these materials, then, scientists can fine-tune the level of conductivity. Because electronics require precise amounts of conductivity and insulation, the development of semiconductors has been instrumental in new technologies.

1. Which of the following would be the best title for this passage?

a. "Insulators and Conductors"
b. "Conductivity"
c. "Charged Gases"
d. "Operation of a Photocopier"

2. Based on the information in the passage, which of the following is most likely a conductor?

a. Wood
b. Aluminum foil
c. Plastic
d. Sand

3. Which of the following statements about conductors is true?

a. The electrons in a conductor can behave almost like a gas.
b. All conductors are pure conductors.
c. Charges tend to cluster at one end of a conductor.
d. Gases cannot be conductors.

4. Ionized plasma is an example of a:

a. Liquid conductor
b. Gaseous conductor
c. Liquid insulator
d. Gaseous insulator

5. What is the main purpose of this passage?

a. To demonstrate why conductors are better than insulators
b. To amuse the reader
c. To describe insulators and conductors
d. To give some examples of insulators and conductors

6. Name the unique feature of selenium that makes it useful in photocopiers.

a. Selenium conducts electricity when it is in gas form.
b. Selenium conducts a charge when light shines on it, but is an insulator in the dark.
c. Selenium can be fused onto paper with heat.
d. Selenium creates an effective seal once the ink is on the page.

7. Materials that are neither insulators nor conductors are known as:

a. Photocopiers
b. Electronics
c. Semi-insulators
d. Semiconductors

Passage #2

The steam engine was one of the inventions that ushered in the era of increased productivity known as the Industrial Revolution. Despite the long history of this device, however, it is still massively useful. In many countries, the majority of the electricity is still produced in steam power plants. These plants operate according to a simple system: fossil fuels (i.e. coal, oil, or gas) are combusted to heat water until it turns into steam. The expansion of this steam creates tremendous pressure inside the turbines, which in turn powers a generator, or even a steam engine coupled with a generator.

Steam power was first used to generate mechanical power in the eighteenth century and to create electricity for communities since 1882. The first steam engines were reciprocating, meaning that the steam flowed in two different directions with each cycle. However, the turbines used today are better, because they are more efficient, and their rotation is smoother. These turbines spin, rather than spinning a rod that then spins the alternator. The result is a more efficient motion that reduces the wear on equipment and eliminates the need for frequent maintenance.

Despite being a somewhat antiquated method of generating electricity, steam power plants still have a few clear advantages. They do not require the use of expensive fuel, and they require much less space than more modern power plants. Moreover, they cost much less to build than other power plants, and they can be built almost anywhere, which means that they can be positioned strategically to minimize transportation costs. A steam power plant can be started and stopped quickly, and it can rapidly respond to differences in demand. A steam power plant is capable of working at its capacity for a very long time.

There are some common problems with steam power plants, however. They cost a great deal to maintain and operate, and they are extremely inefficient. A steam power plant typically operates at only about 30% efficiency: the majority of the heat generated through combustion is lost during its passage through the various channels of operation. Furthermore, steam power plants require a huge amount of water, which means that they usually must be placed near bodies of water. These plants also produce large quantities of ash, which may create disposal complications. Finally, the process of constructing a steam power plant can take a long time.

8. What is the primary intention of this passage?

a. To advocate the construction of more steam power plants
b. To amuse the reader with a story about steam engines
c. To explain the origins of the Industrial Revolution
d. To describe how steam is used to generate power

9. Which of the following would be the best location for a steam power plant?

a. A large pond alongside a major highway
b. A major city
c. An isolated lake at high altitude
d. A swamp near an airport

10. With regard to steam engines, what does "reciprocating" mean?

a. The engines require less water.
b. Steam flows in two different directions.
c. The steam emerges from two different holes.
d. The engine requires frequent lubrication.

11. Which of the following is NOT a major disadvantage of steam power plants?

a. Steam power plants require expensive fuel.
b. Steam power plants are expensive to operate.
c. Steam power plants require a huge amount of water
d. Steam power plants lose most of the heat they generate through combustion.

12. Who would be the most likely intended audience for this passage?

a. Experienced engineers
b. General public
c. School teachers
d. Children

13. Which of the following sentences best illustrates the efficiency of a steam power plant?

a. "Furthermore, steam power plants require a huge amount of water, which means that they usually must be placed near bodies of water."
b. "These plants also produce large quantities of ash, which may create disposal complications."
c. "A steam power plant can be started and stopped quickly, and it can rapidly respond to differences in demand."
d. "Despite being a somewhat antiquated method of generating electricity, steam power plants still have a few clear advantages."

Passage #3

In most cases, the transfer of heat requires a medium, like air, water, or metal. Radiation, however, can occur without a medium. Radiation is the movement of energy through electromagnetic waves. Most people know that excessive radiation can be harmful, but very few are aware that most of the radiation absorbed by an average person comes from natural sources. In the United States, an average person receives approximately 0.2 rem (roentgen equivalent for man, a unit that takes into account the amount and the type of radiation); of this, only about 20% comes from human activities. The rest comes from natural sources, like rocks, minerals, and even cosmic rays from outer space.

Nevertheless, there are health risks associated with excessive exposure to radioactive materials. The risk is not restricted to the production of nuclear power, either. People who fly a great deal, or even just live at a high elevation, are more susceptible to radiation originating beyond the earth's atmosphere. Medical personnel are often exposed to greater levels of radiation because of the chemicals and equipment (x rays, for instance) they use.

Another common source of dangerous radiation is radon gas, which may seep up from the ground and into the foundations of a house. Radon gas has a very short half-life, and it decays in the lungs into a radioactive isotope of polonium. This polonium can stay in the lungs for a long time, and while it is there, it can contribute to cancerous mutations in the tissue. Every year, more than 15,000 people in the United States die of lung cancer caused by radon. Certain types of soil and bedrock are particularly prone to radon, but they are distributed throughout the country. A recent study by the Environmental Protection Agency estimated that one in every fifteen homes has elevated levels of radon.

Radon problems can be identified with a simple test, and there are some other ways to protect against excessive exposure to radiation. A great deal of radiation is blocked by skin and clothing, but some particles are still inhaled and ingested. Radioactive particles may penetrate the skin, though rarely far enough to damage the internal organs. The most powerful radioactive particles, however, can only be stopped by concrete or lead.

14. Which of the following would be the best title for this passage?

a. "Heat Transfer"
b. "The Dangers of Radon"
c. "Healthy Radiation"
d. "The Dangers of Radiation"

15. With regard to radiation, what does "rem" mean?

a. Radiation enhancement material
b. Roentgen equivalent for man
c. Radon equivalent mixture
d. Rapid eye movement

16. Why are medical personnel more likely to be exposed to harmful levels of radiation?

a. Because of the chemicals they use in their work
b. Because of their exposure to body fluids
c. Because of their higher rates of obesity
d. Because of the elevation at which they work

17. Which of the following people would be most susceptible to radiation from outer space?

a. Sea captain
b. Nuclear engineer
c. Taxi driver
d. Airline pilot

18. Which harmful gas is often found in the foundations of houses?

a. Radium
b. Carbon dioxide
c. Radon
d. Helium

19. In the lungs, radon gas can turn into:

a. Cancer
b. Radium
c. Polonium
d. Neutrons

20. What does it mean that radon gas has a "very short half-life"?

a. It is radioactive.
b. It decays quickly.
c. It cannot be contained.
d. It collects under houses.

21. Why is it problematic for the types of soil that are prone to radon to be distributed throughout the country?

a. It is more difficult to predict where radon hazards will exist.
b. It is more difficult to remove these types of soil.
c. It is easier for this soil to escape notice.
d. Radon has a very short half-life.

Passage #4

It is certain that there would be more coal consumed in conventional boilers, if it were it not for harmful emissions. The combustion of coal releases sulphur dioxide, carbon dioxide, and several nitrogen dioxides, among other chemical gases. These chemicals have adverse consequences for human health and for the environment.

One possible solution to this problem is the technique known as carbon sequestration, the injection of carbon dioxide into geologic formations far below the earth's surface. There are a number of possible destinations for sequestered carbon: the bottom of the ocean, sandstone formations, and partially empty oil and gas reservoirs. In some cases, the carbon dioxide is compressed before it is pumped to its new home. There is a great deal of optimism about carbon sequestration at present: a report by the United Nations recently suggested that more than half of global carbon emissions could be disposed of in this way.

There are other technologies that inspire hopes of mitigating the harmful impact of greenhouse gases. For instance, China has become the leading user of supercritical boilers, which, contrary to their name, actually get so hot that water passes immediately from liquid to gas form without boiling at all. The speed with which steam is generated by these devices reduces the amount of coal required to heat them, thus reducing dangerous emissions.

Another possible method for reducing carbon emissions is to combine biomass crops with coal in power plants. The addition of biomass, which is any material created from the remains of plants or animals, reduces the emission of carbon dioxide. Many experts believe that so-called "flex fuel" boilers, designed to handle this mixture of materials, can be used effectively until more permanent sources of renewable energy have been developed.

Finally, scientists have developed the integrated gasification combined cycle, or IGCC, which converts coal into gas and then purifies this gas prior to combustion. The IGCC not only removes pollutants, it also preserves them in such a way that many of them can be used in other industrial processes. The technology used in the IGCC can also convert the carbon in the gas to hydrogen, and the carbon dioxide produced by this conversion can be contained and stored. At present, this technology is in the trial phase, but it offers real hope of reducing pollution without crippling the coal industry.

22. A good title for this passage would be:

a. "Coal and You"
b. "The Rise of Clean Coal Technology"
c. "Carbon Sequestration and Biomass"
d. "The Environmental Impact of Coal"

23. Which of the following is NOT a possible destination for sequestered carbon?

a. Sandstone formations
b. The bottom of the ocean
c. Unused silos
d. Gas reservoirs

24. Which country has become the leading user of supercritical boilers?

a. Brazil
b. United States
c. China
d. Japan

25. What is the best definition for *mitigating* in the first sentence of the third paragraph?

a. Diminishing
b. Catalyzing
c. Increasing
d. Altering

26. The water in a supercritical boiler passes from liquid to gas without:

a. Burning
b. Expanding
c. Heating
d. Boiling

27. The remains of plants and animals are called:

a. Ecomass
b. Biofuel
c. Ecofuel
d. Biomass

28. Which of the following statements about the integrated gasification combined cycle is false?

a. The IGCC can be used to eliminate carbon from gas.
b. The IGCC is in use around the United States.
c. The IGCC can reduce carbon dioxide emissions.
d. The IGCC produces purified gas.

Passage #5

As the need for electrical power grows and the supply of available fossil fuels dwindles, nuclear power plants have become increasingly popular globally. Nuclear power plants generate energy through a process known as nuclear fission. Inside a nuclear reactor, the altering of nuclear particles releases huge amounts of energy, as some of the mass of the nuclei is actually converted into energy. Nuclear power plants were thought to be the future of energy production in the United States in the 1960s and 1970s, but high-profile accidents and unanticipated expenses tarnished their image. Nuclear power is more popular in countries like Japan, India, and France.

Nuclear power plants have some obvious advantages over other methods of generating electricity. For one thing, they require very little fuel, which eliminates all of the costs and hassles associated with acquiring, moving, and storing large amounts of coal or gas. A nuclear power plant can supply much more power than a steam plant of the same size and, indeed, is the most space-efficient type of power plant. The use of nuclear power plants conserves the supply of other fossil fuels, which can then be used as raw material in chemical industries. Finally, it is very easy to adjust the output of a nuclear power plant, so it is easy to achieve maximum efficiency.

These plants have their drawbacks, however, some of which are well known to the general public. Nuclear power plants cost a huge amount of money to build, and their construction, operation, and maintenance require the highest level of technical skill and expertise. The operation of a nuclear power plant is relatively cheap, but the cost of maintenance can be astronomical. Finally, of course, there is always the risk of a catastrophic accident at a nuclear power plant. The presence of extremely radioactive material presents a serious hazard for any people or wildlife in the area. These accidents are very rare, but when they occur they are devastating.

The selection of a site for a nuclear power plant is subject to some unique considerations. The best spot for one of these plants is next to a body of water and away from any populated areas. The water is important for cooling the plant during operation. It is also beneficial for the plant to be easily reachable by some form of transportation, as construction will require a great deal of material and equipment to be moved.

29. Which of the following best describes this passage?

a. A description of nuclear power plants
b. An argument in favor of nuclear power
c. A guide to selecting a site for a nuclear power plant
d. An argument against nuclear power

30. What is the name of the process through which a nuclear reactor creates energy?

a. Fusion
b. Propulsion
c. Fission
d. Reaction

31. The second paragraph of the passage deals primarily with:

a. The hazards of radioactive material
b. The advantages of nuclear power plants
c. The materials used in a nuclear power plant
d. The selection of a site for a nuclear power plant

32. In which of the following countries has nuclear power become less popular?

a. United States
b. France
c. Japan
d. India

33. Which of the following is an advantage of nuclear power plants?

a. They do not require skilled personnel.
b. They are inexpensive to construct.
c. They are inexpensive to maintain.
d. They are efficient relative to the amount of space they require.

34. Why is it easy for a nuclear power plant to run efficiently?

a. Because the output can be adjusted easily
b. Because operation does not require skilled employees
c. Because the plants are far from population centers
d. Because nuclear power has become less popular

35. Based on the information in the passage, which of the following is probably true?

a. Nuclear power will become more popular in the United States.
b. Nuclear accidents cannot be prevented in every possible case.
c. The nuclear plants of the future will be near large cities.
d. Some wildlife benefit from exposure to radioactive material.

36. Which of the following is the topic sentence of the last paragraph?

a. "The selection of a site for a nuclear power plant is subject to some unique considerations."
b. "It is also beneficial for the plant to be easily reachable by some form of transportation, as construction will require a great deal of material and equipment to be moved."
c. "The water is important for cooling the plant during operation."
d. "The best spot for one of these plants is next to a body of water and away from any populated areas."

Assembling Objects

For this practice test section, assume that shapes may be rotated but not reflected.

1. Which of the following configurations represents how the following object might appear if its components are rearranged?

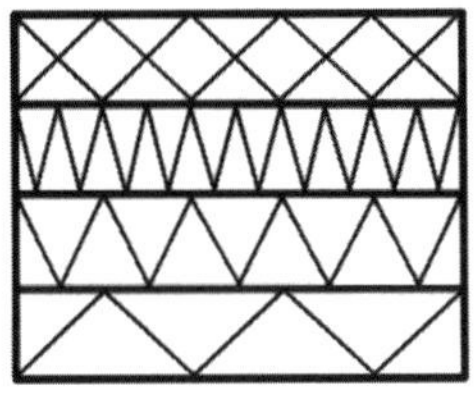

a. 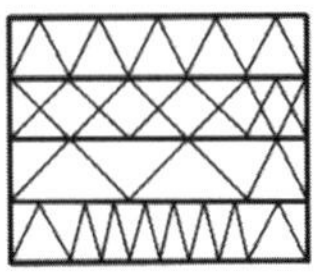 b. 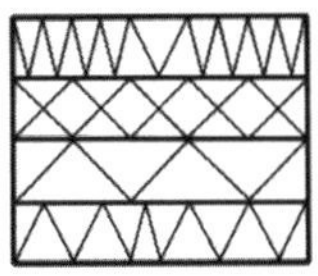 c. 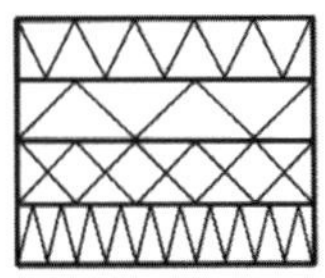 d. 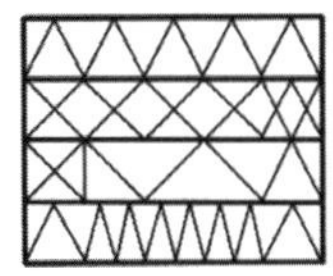

2. Which of the following configurations represents how the following objects might appear if they are rearranged?

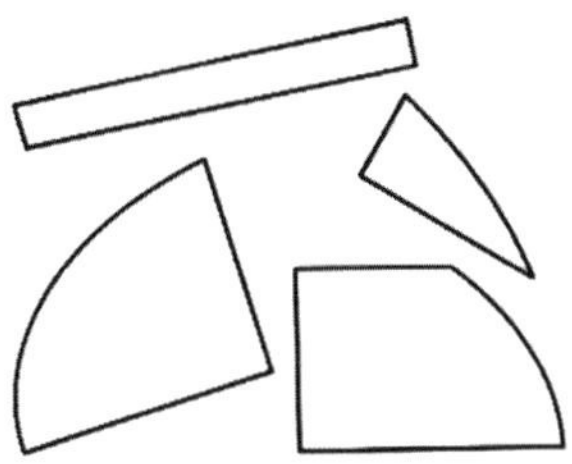

a. 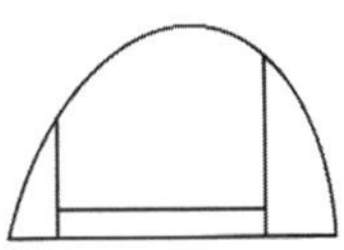 b. 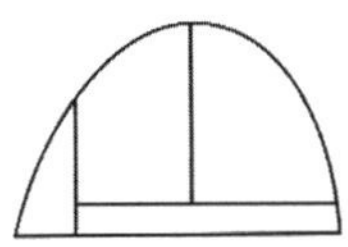 c. 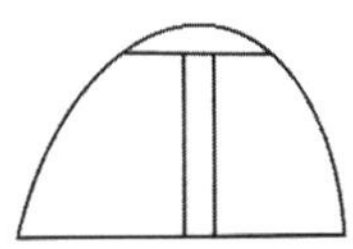 d. 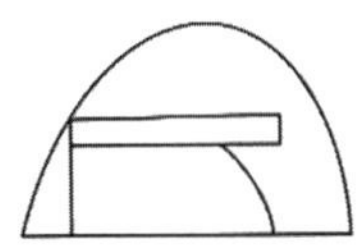

3. Which of the following configurations represents how the following objects might appear if they are rearranged?

a. 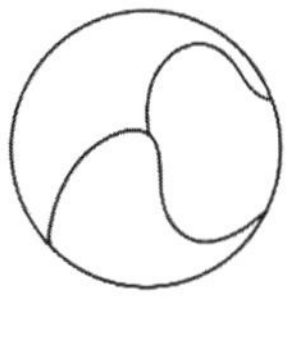 b.  c. 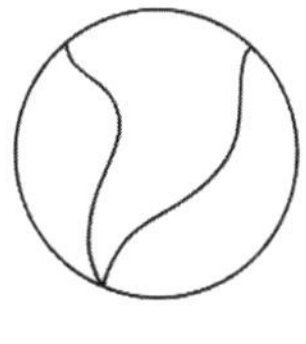 d. 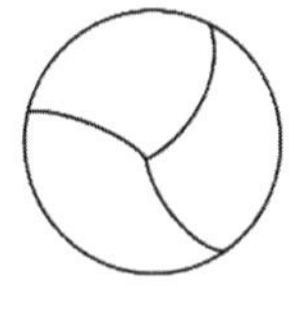

4. Which of the following configurations represents how the following object might appear if its components are rearranged?

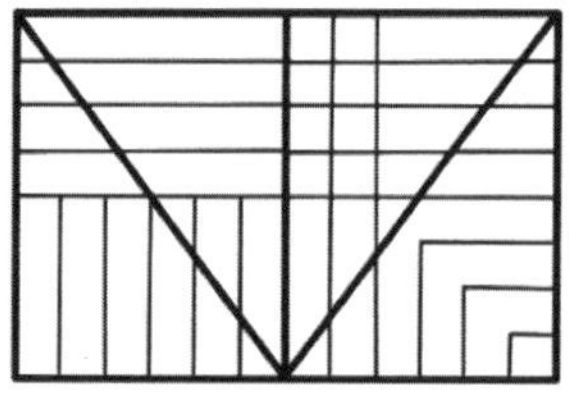

a. 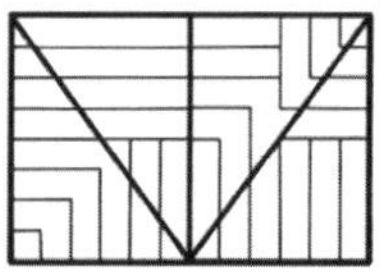 b. 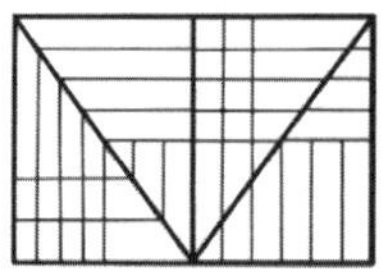 c. 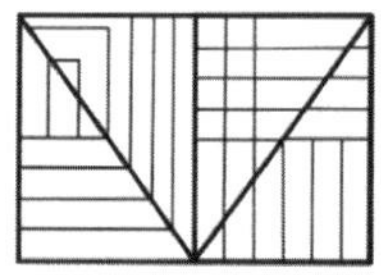 d. 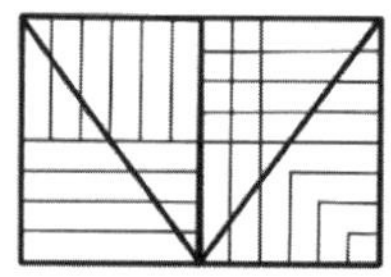

5. Which of the following configurations represents how the following objects might appear if they are rearranged?

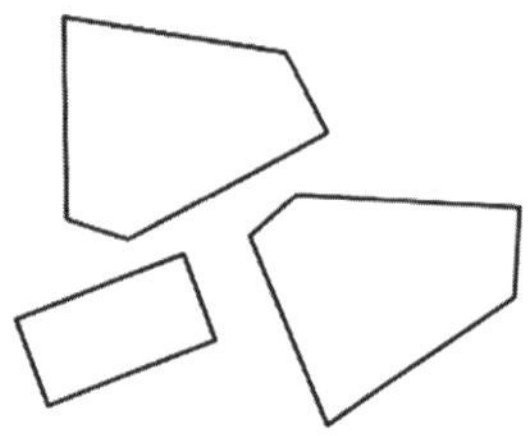

a. 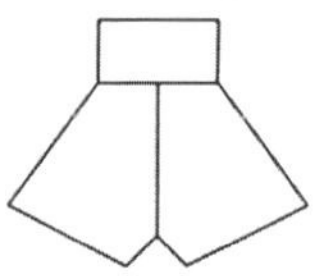 b. 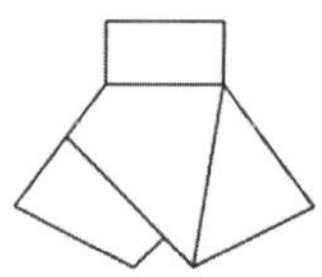 c. 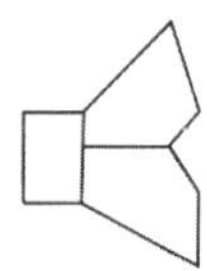 d. 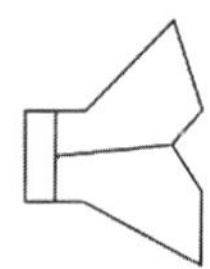

6. Which figure is a vertical reflection or flip of the object shown?

a. 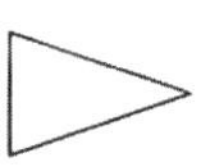 b.  c.  d. 

7. Which of the following configurations represents how the following object might appear if its components are rearranged?

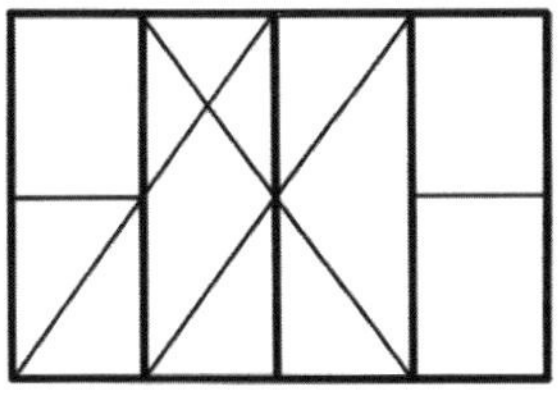

a. 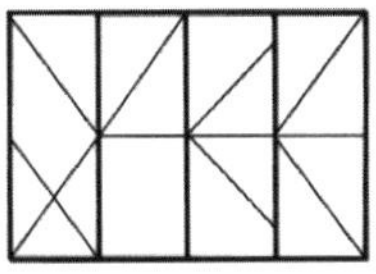 b. 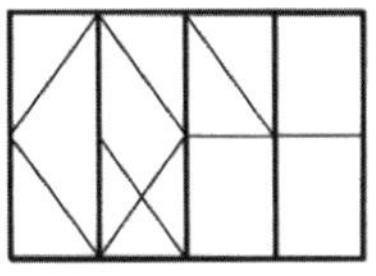 c. 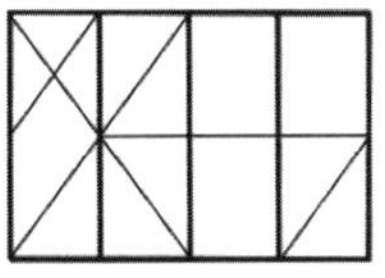 d. 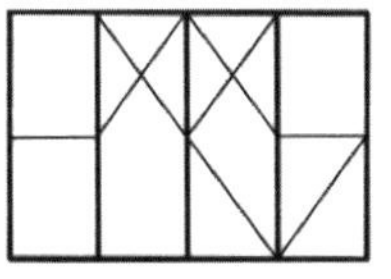

8. If the objects below are translated along the path indicated by the line, keeping in mind that a dotted line corresponds to a place on the side of the object that cannot be seen, how might the final image appear? (Note: the images may not be rotated.)

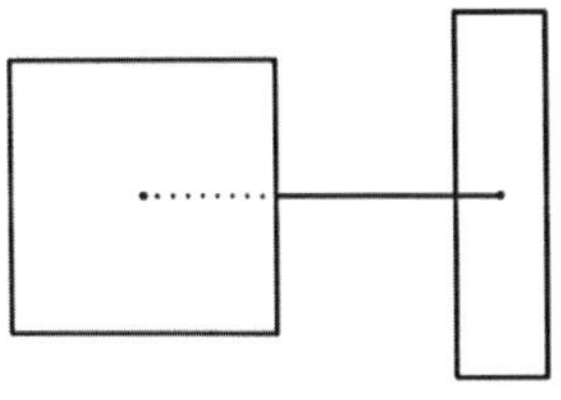

a. 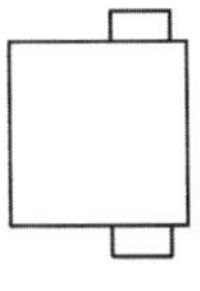 b. 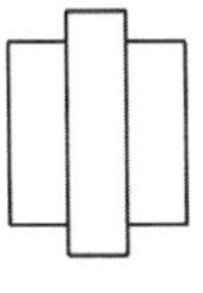 c. 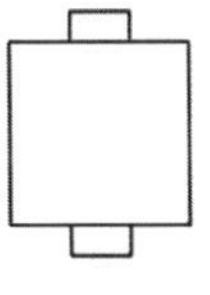 d. 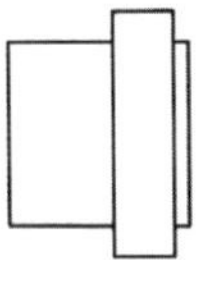

9. Which of the following configurations represents how the following objects might appear if they are rearranged?

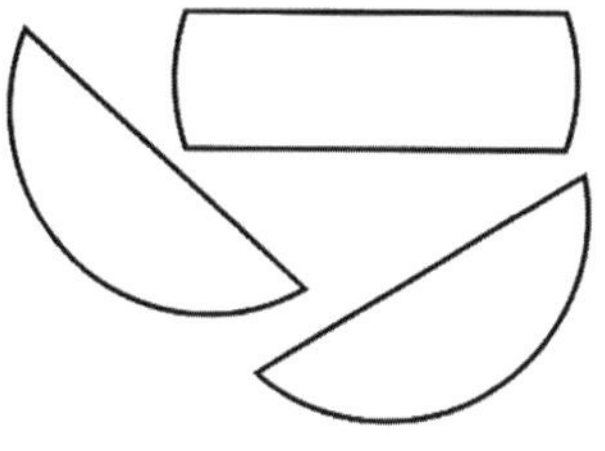

a. 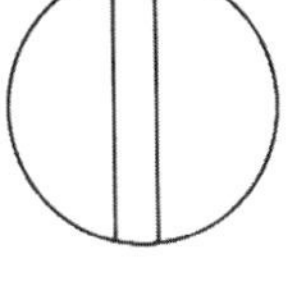 b. 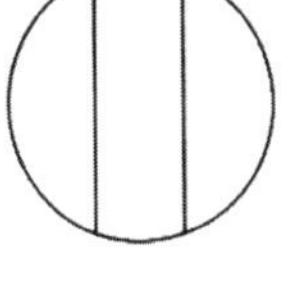 c. 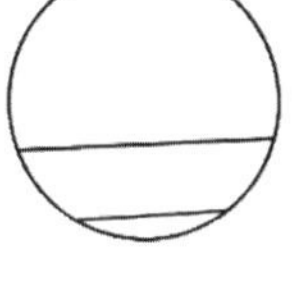 d. 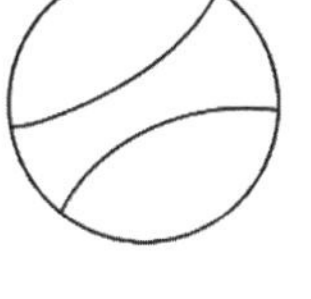

10. Which of the following configurations represents how the following objects might appear if they are rearranged?

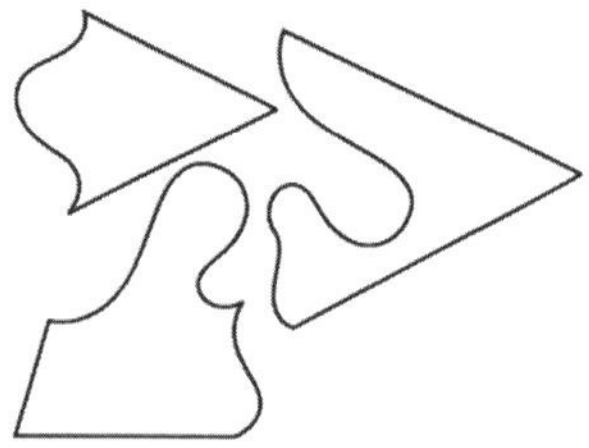

a. 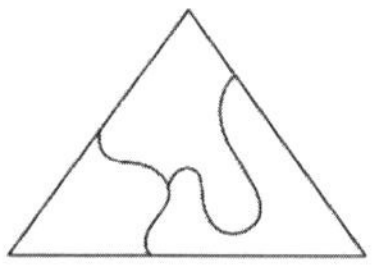 b. 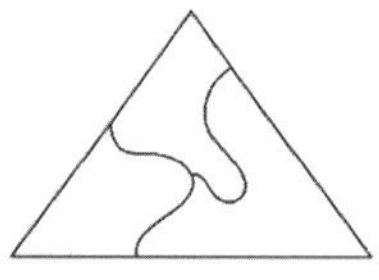 c. 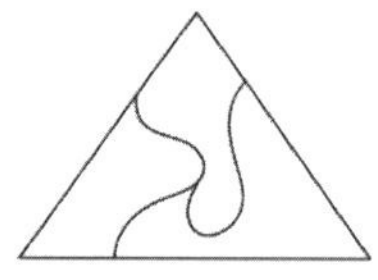 d. 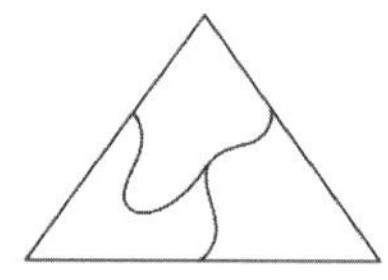

11. If the objects below are translated along the path indicated by the line, keeping in mind that a dotted line corresponds to a place on the side of the object that cannot be seen, how might the final image appear? (Note: the images may not be rotated.)

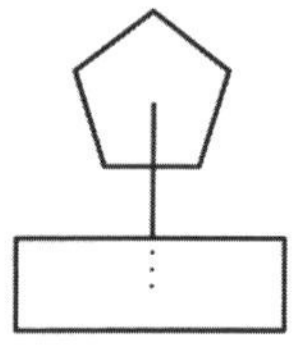

a. 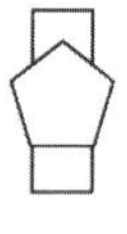 b.  c. 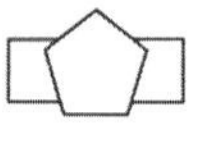 d. 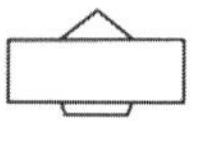

12. Which figure is a horizontal reflection or flip of the object shown?

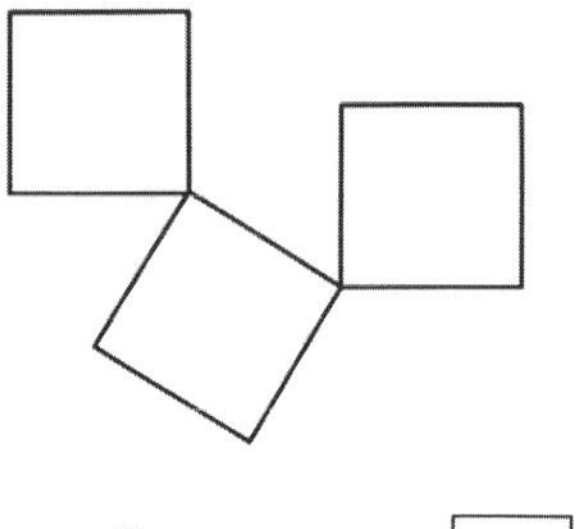

a. 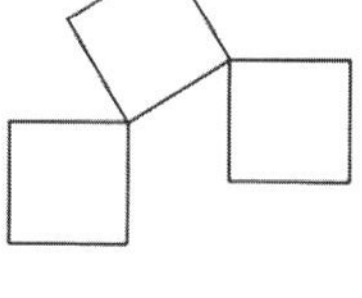 b. 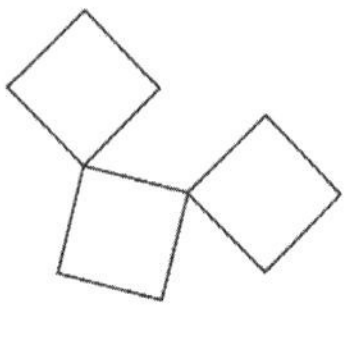 c. 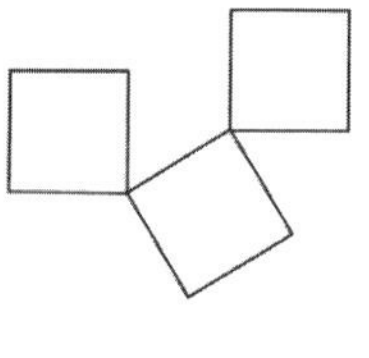 d. 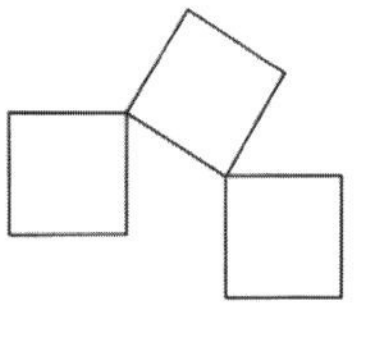

13. Which of the following configurations represents how the following objects might appear if they are rearranged?

a. 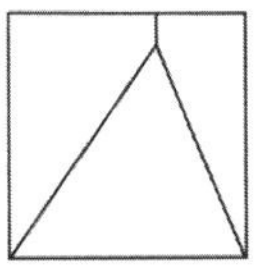 b. 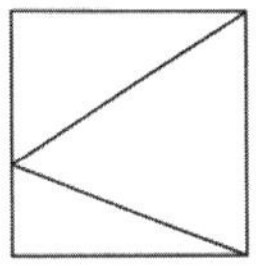 c. 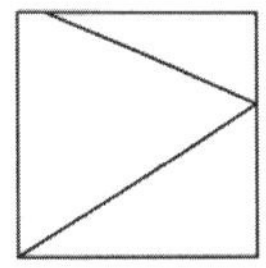 d. 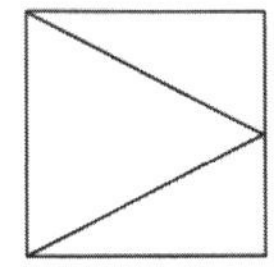

14. Which of the following configurations represents how the following object might appear if its components are rearranged?

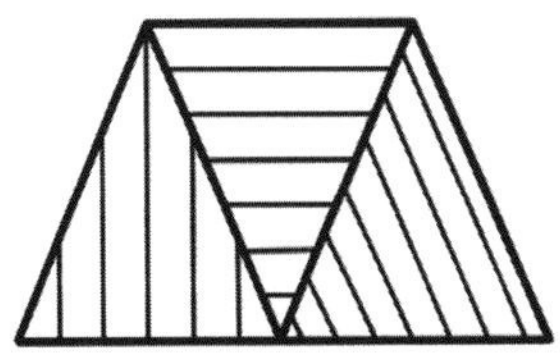

a. 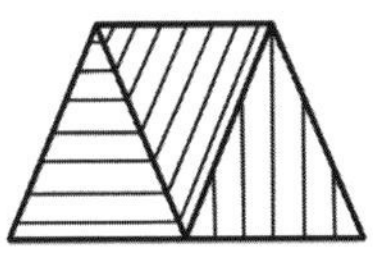 b. 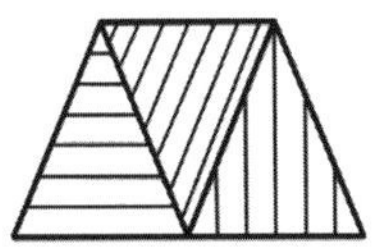 c. 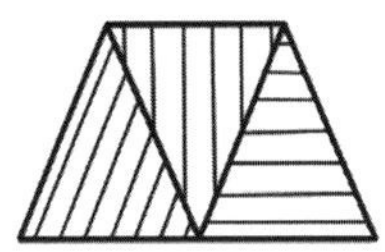 d. 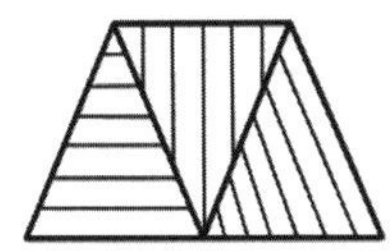

15. Which of the following configurations represents how the following objects might appear if they are rearranged?

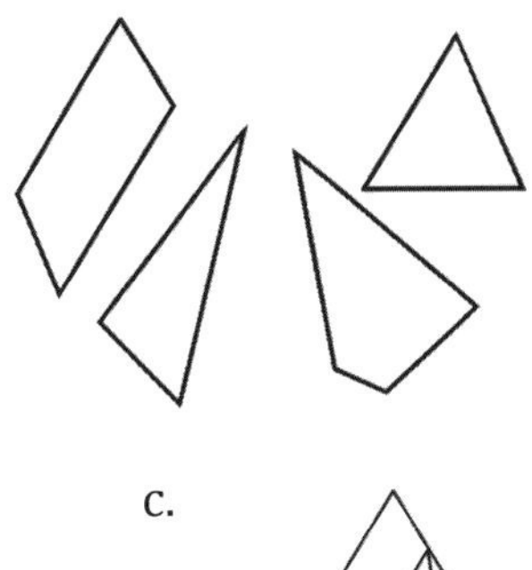

a. 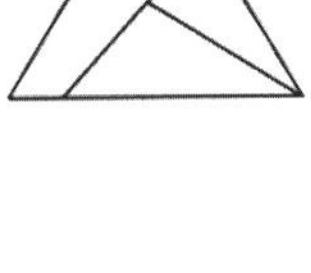 b. 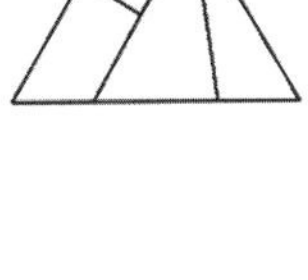 c. 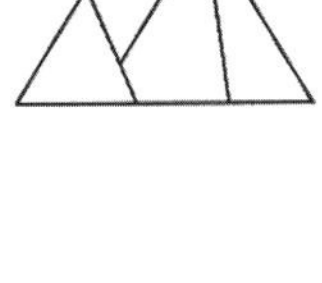 d. 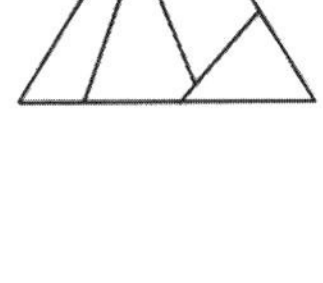

16. Which of the following configurations represents how the following object might appear if its components are rearranged?

a. 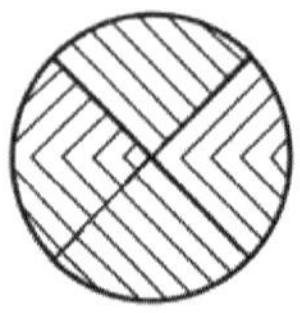 b.  c.  d. 

17. Which figure best represents what might result if the shapes shown on the left are cut out of the shape on the right?

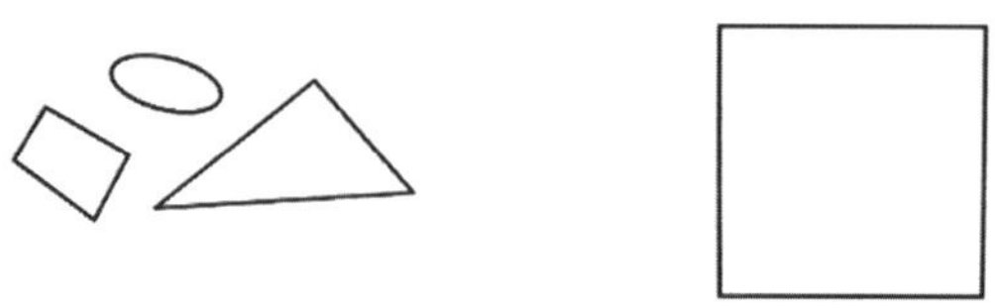

a.  b. 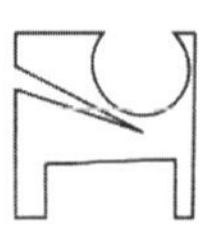 c.  d. 

18. Which figure best shows how the objects might be connected if a line is drawn from one point to the other?

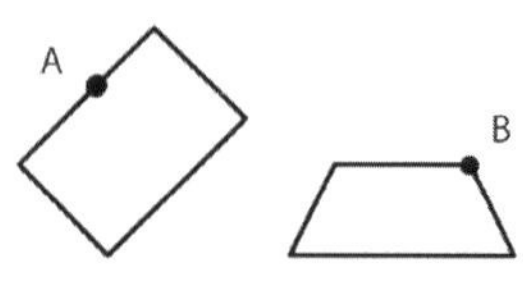

a. 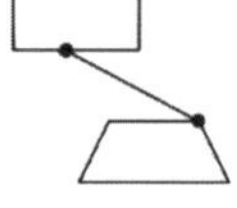 b. 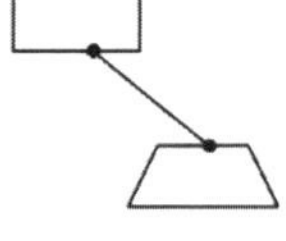 c. 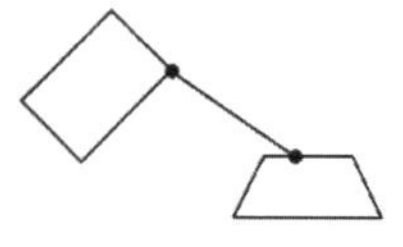 d. 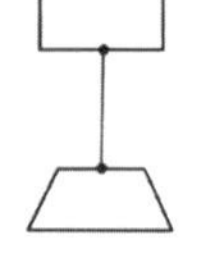

19. Which objects were cut out of a rectangle to form this image?

a. 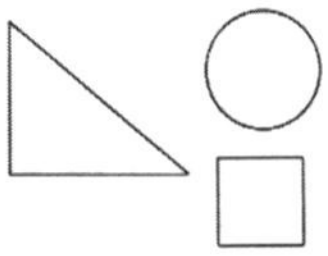 b. 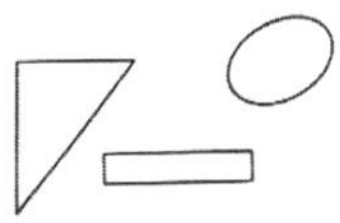 c. 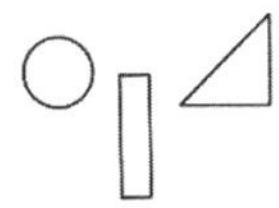 d. 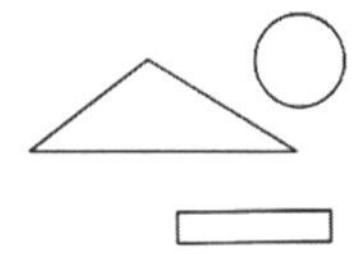

20. Which figure best shows how the objects might be connected if a line is drawn from one point to the other?

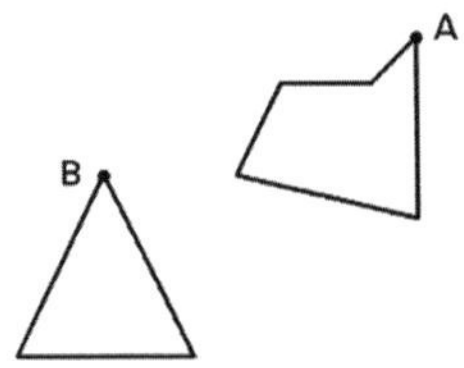

a. 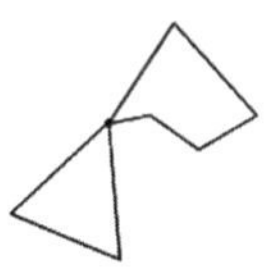 b.  c. 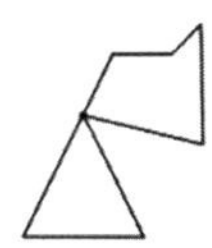 d. 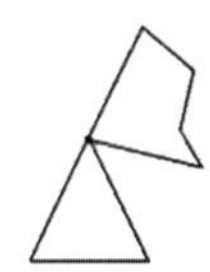

Mechanical Concepts

This is a test of your ability to understand mechanical concepts. Each question has a picture, a question and three possible answers. Read each question carefully, study the picture, and decide which answer is correct.

1. Two motors are used to pull crates of gold bars up a hill. Which hillside (A or B) will be easier to pull on? (If equal, mark C)

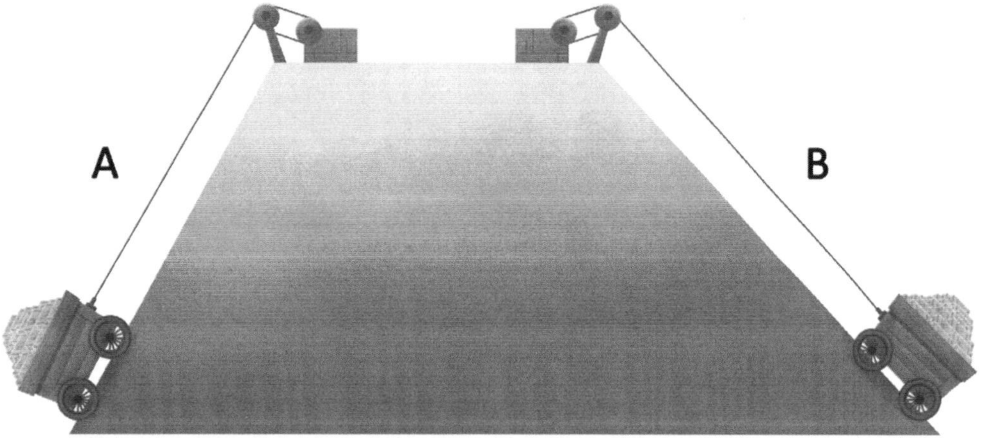

2. A weight can be lifted by one pulley or by four pulleys. Which will require less pulling force? (If equal, mark C)

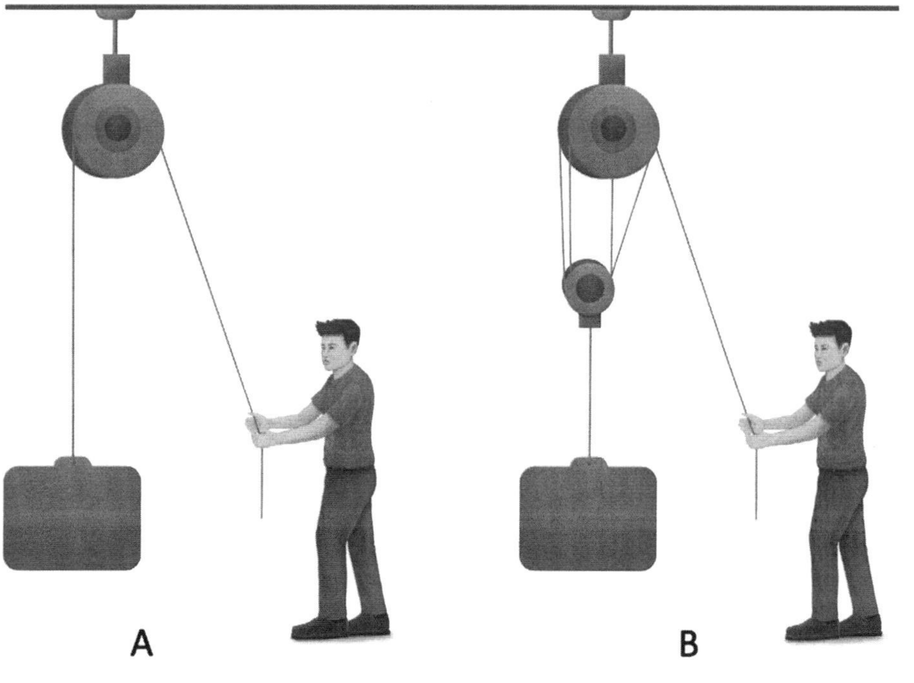

3. Four gears rotate together. Gear 1 spins clockwise. A gear is added. In the new set of five gears, will Gear 2 spin clockwise (A), counterclockwise (B), or not at all (C)?

4. Two identical blocks of clay are suspended from the ceiling by strings. They are raised to different heights and dropped towards each other. After they hit and stick together, where will the new mass of clay go—left (A), right (B), or nowhere (C)?

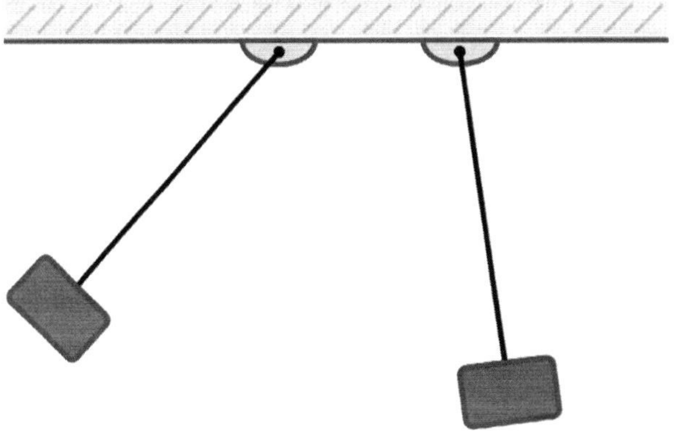

5. Water flows through a funnel. With reference to the large end, will the small end have greater water speed (A), lower water speed (B), or the same water speed (C)?

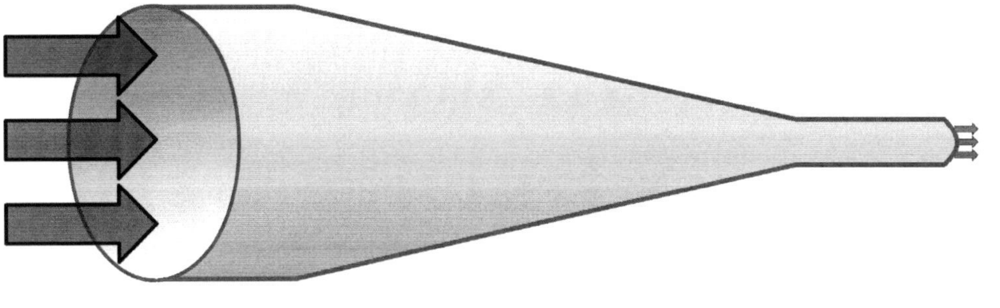

6. Two identical blocks are released from the same height down two separate slopes of identical length. Slope A is made of grass and Slope B is made of ice. If both blocks are released at the same time, which block will reach the bottom first? (If equal, mark C)

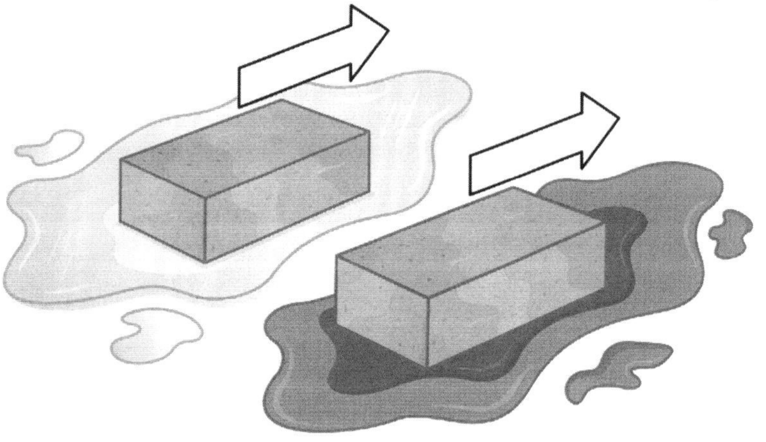

7. Two identical gas tanks have oxygen inside. One has twice the mass of oxygen as the other. Does the one with less mass have more pressure (A), less pressure (B), or the same pressure as the other (C)?

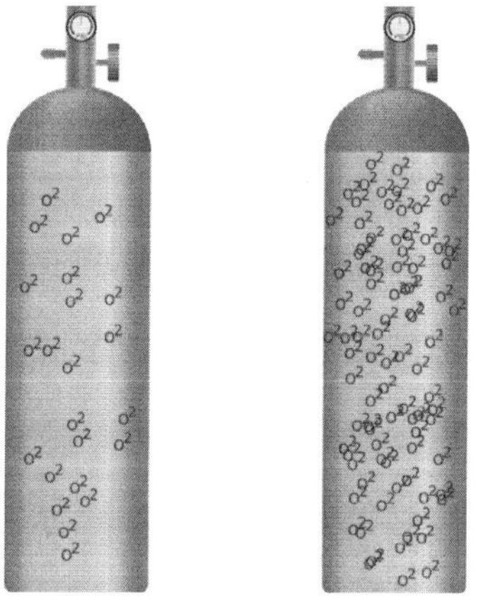

8. In this set of belts and pulleys, which pulley is rotating with the lowest number of revolutions per minute?

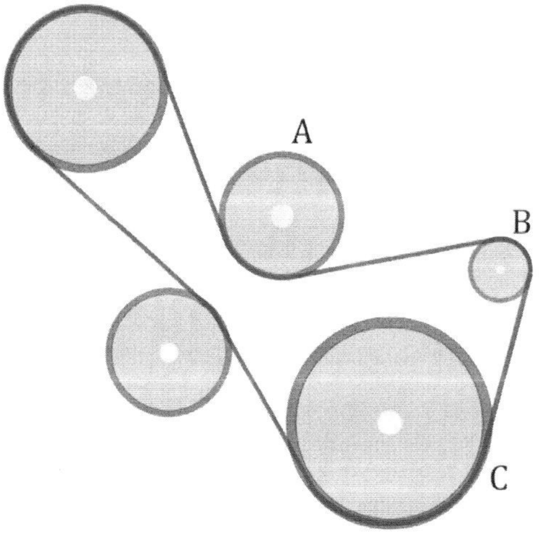

9. A farmer wants to put a heavy barrel in front of his gate to keep it shut. Which location will keep the gate closed best?

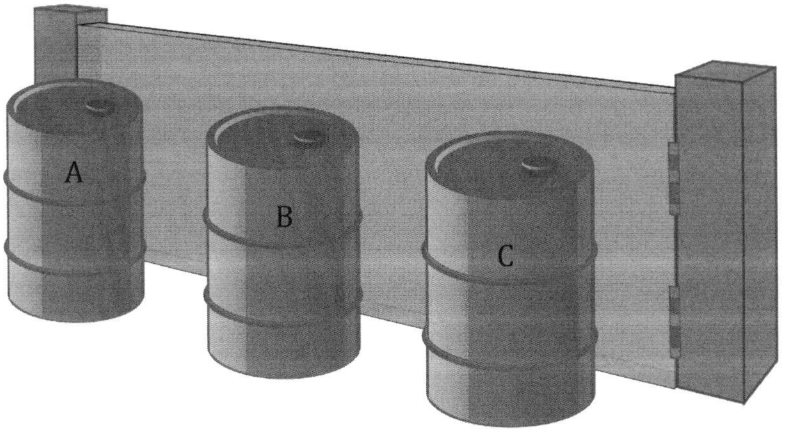

10. A soccer player kicks a ball up into the air from the ground. Ignoring air resistance, when the ball hits the ground, will it be going slower (A), faster (B), or the same speed (C) as when it was kicked?

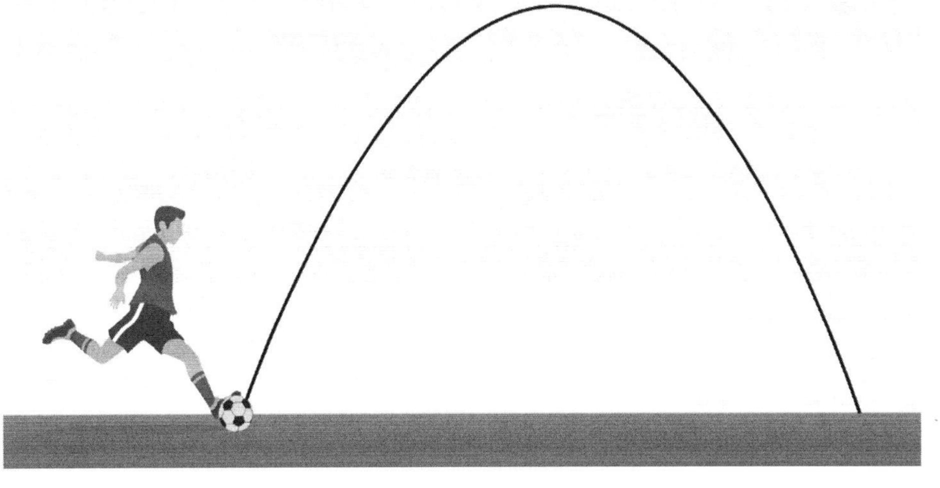

11. Two men are trying to lift identical rocks with levers. Will the man with the longer lever need to push with a larger force (A), a smaller force (B), or the same force (C) as the man with the shorter lever to lift the rock?

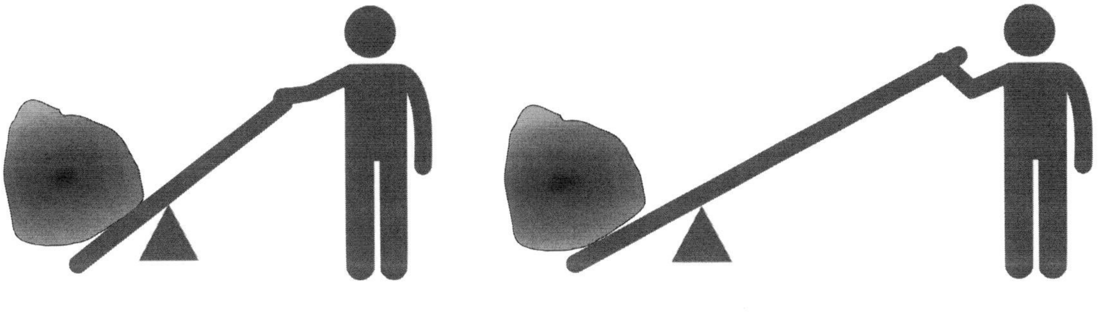

12. Which switch should be closed to turn on the light?

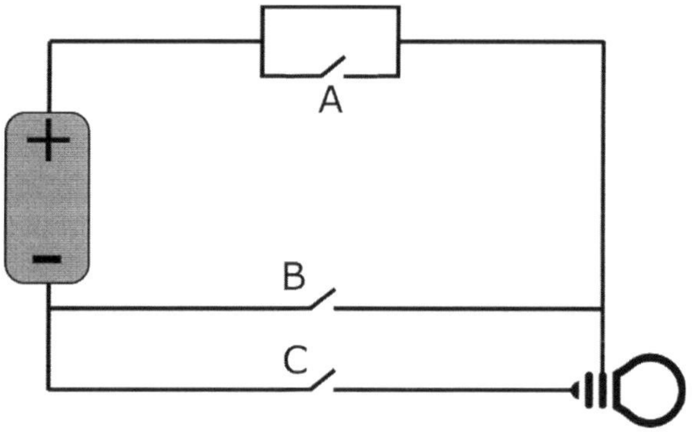

13. Two boats support a bridge. When the truck is at the position indicated, which boat is supporting more weight? (If equal, mark C)

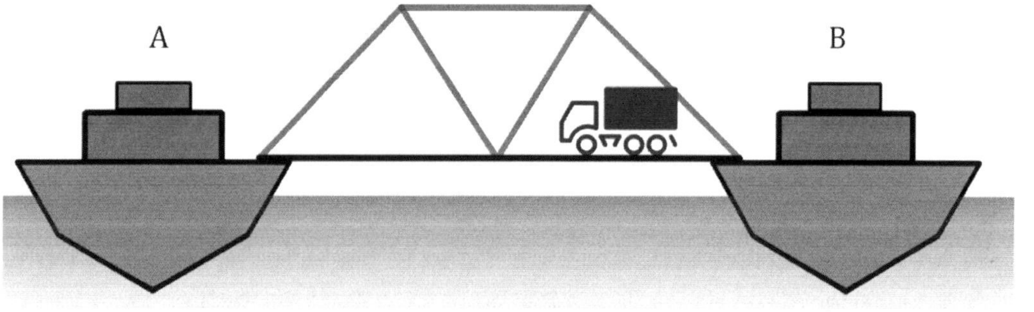

14. Two machetes are used to clear tall grass. Which machete will allow for the fastest cutting? (If equal, mark C)

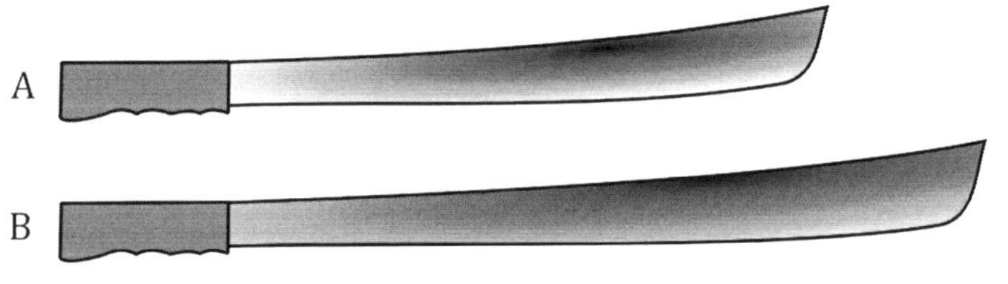

15. Will adding salt to water make objects in the water more likely to float (A) or less likely to float (B)? (If equal, mark C)

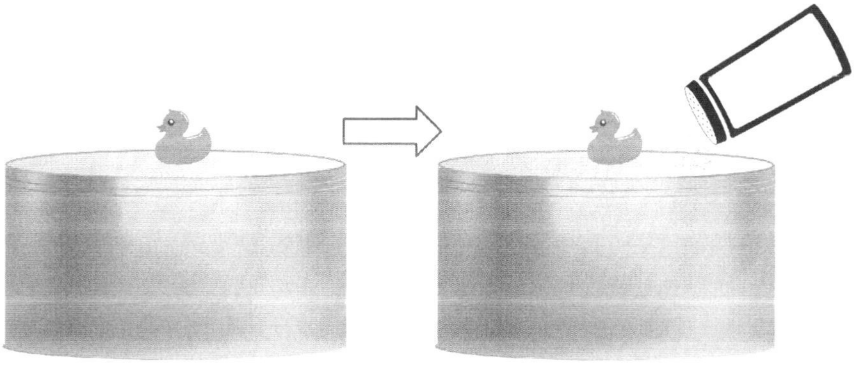

16. Will adding water to a water tower increase (A), decrease (B), or not affect (C) the water pressure at the bottom of the water tower?

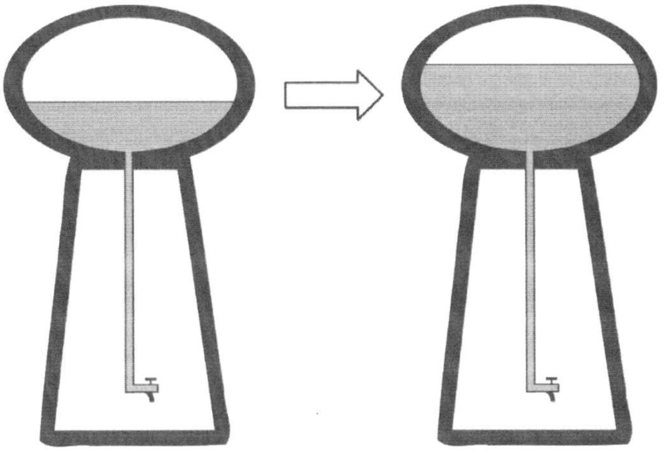

17. A man wants to cool down by getting into the river. Which location will cool him down the fastest?

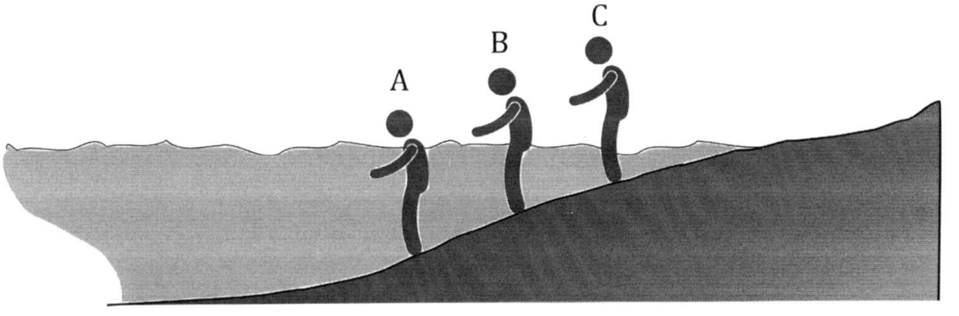

18. Milk is measured in a liquid measuring cup. Which orientation will allow for the most accurate reading of the volume of milk?

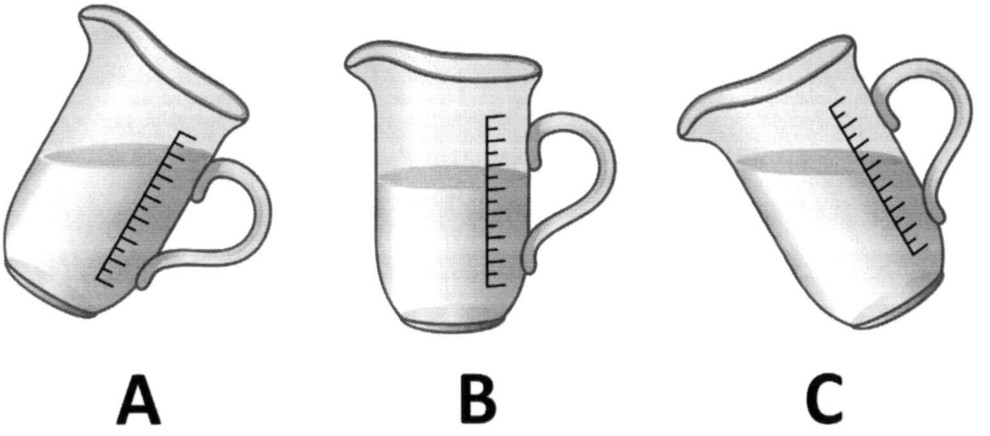

19. Two vehicles weigh the same. Which is more likely to tip on a corner? (If equal, mark C)

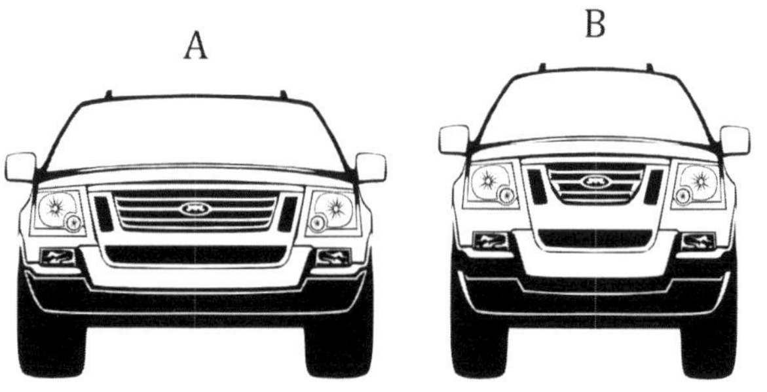

20. A bucket has a clear tube on the outside which connects at the bottom. How high will the fluid in the tube go?

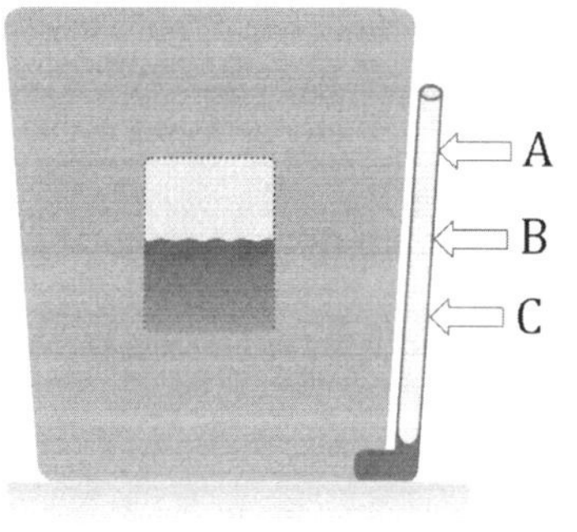

21. Two identical balls are pushed vertically into identical springs. After the balls are released, which ball will reach the greatest height? (If equal, mark C)

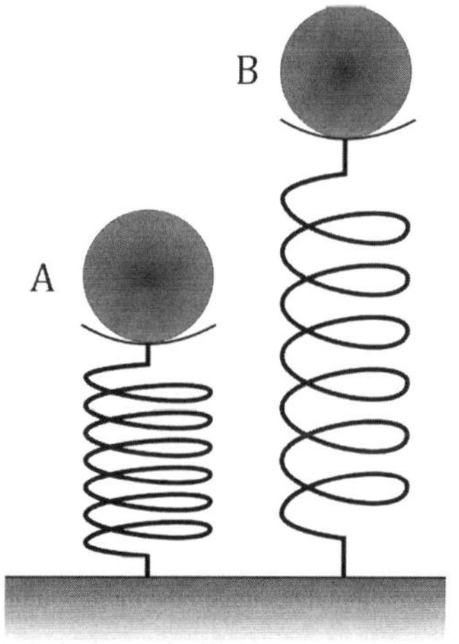

22. A fan spins with a certain rotational speed. Which part of the fan blade will travel the fastest through the air?

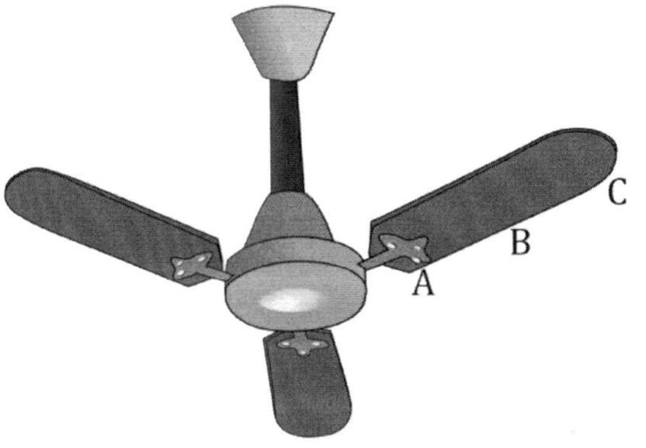

23. Two bags of sand are poured into identical tanks of water. Which tank will have the highest water level? (If equal, mark C)

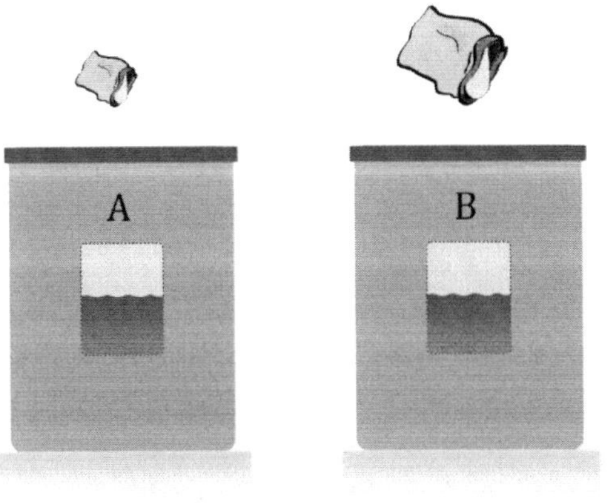

24. Two identical balls with identical speeds bounce off each other. Which path is ball 1 likely to follow?

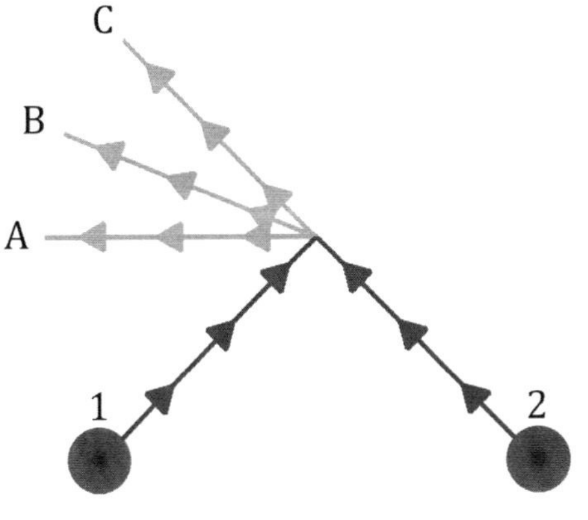

25. A pendulum is released at the shown height. It travels to point B. After the pendulum swings back and forth four times, how high is the pendulum likely to reach?

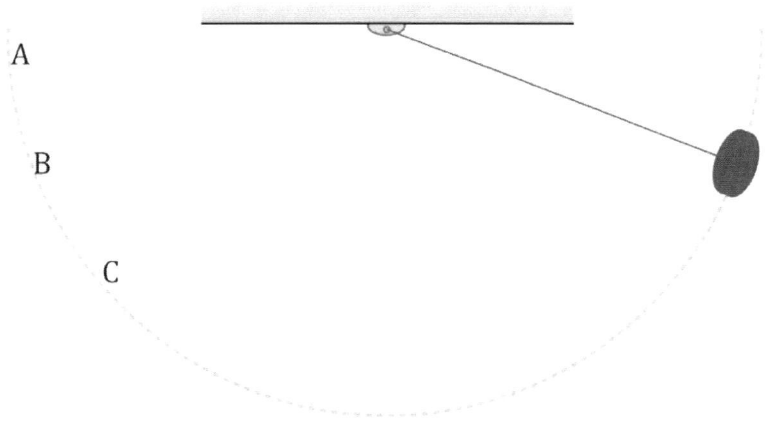

26. A sack of concrete is on a board. If the man lifts the board on the end to raise the concrete, where should the concrete be located to minimize the required force?

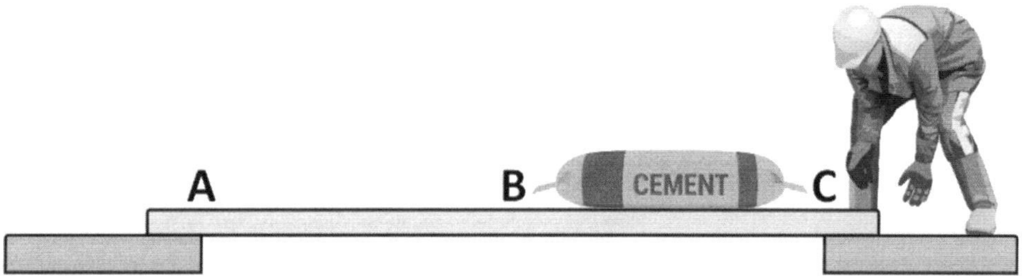

27. Two bowling balls are dropped onto identical springs. One bowling ball is dropped from 5 feet. The other is dropped from 10 feet. Which spring will compress more? (If equal, mark C)

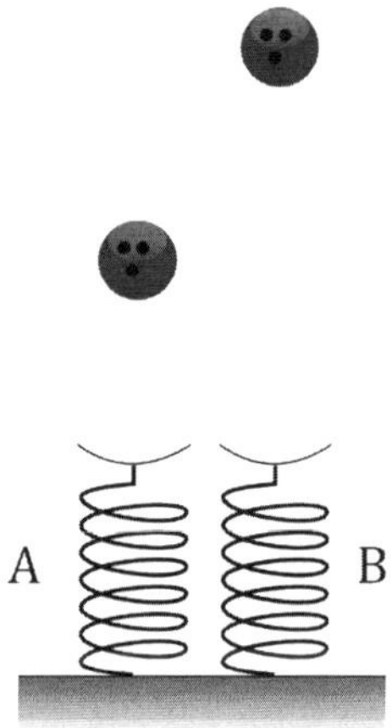

28. A toddler pulls the toilet paper off a toilet paper roll with a constant speed. Will the roll spin faster when the roll is small (A) or when the roll is large (B)? (If equal, mark C)

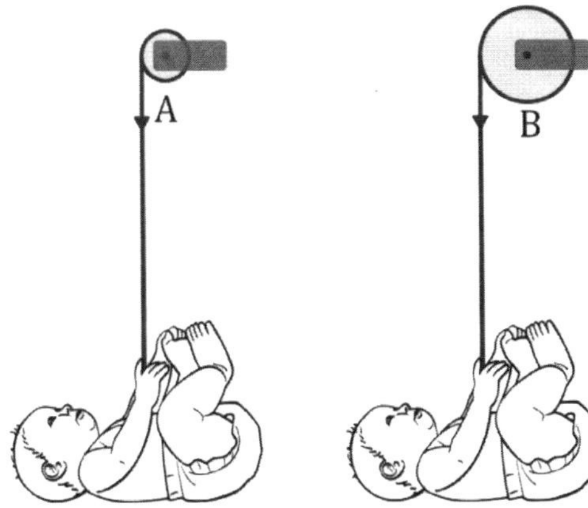

29. Where will the water travel fastest through the pipe? (If equal, mark C)

30. A bowling ball and a baseball are dropped from the same height onto separate platforms. Assuming negligible air resistance, where should the platform be placed so that the bowling ball and baseball land at the same time?

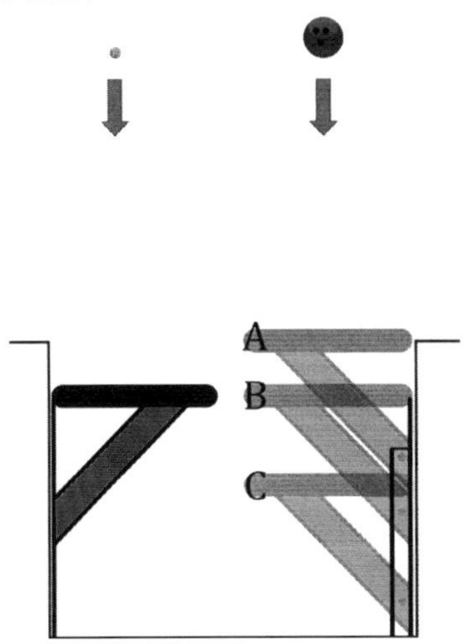

31. A boy spins a ball with a string. If he suddenly releases the string, which direction will the ball travel?

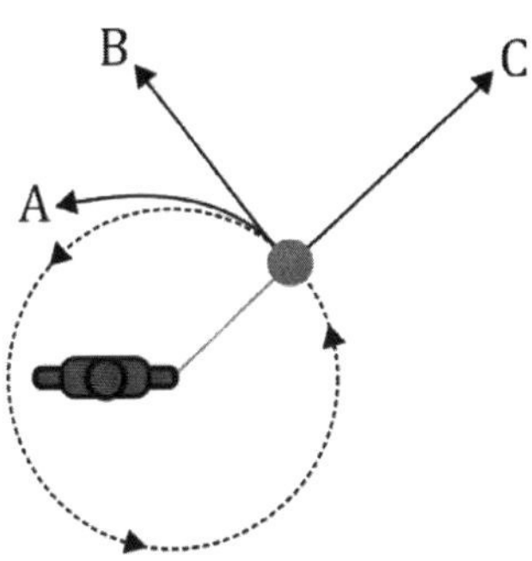

32. An antique bicycle has one large wheel and one small wheel. When the bicycle is moving forward, which wheel rotates faster or do they rotate at the same speed? (If equal, mark C)

33. A cart has a bucket of water resting on it. If the cart needs to make a right turn quickly, which direction of road tilt would help keep the bucket as stable as possible?

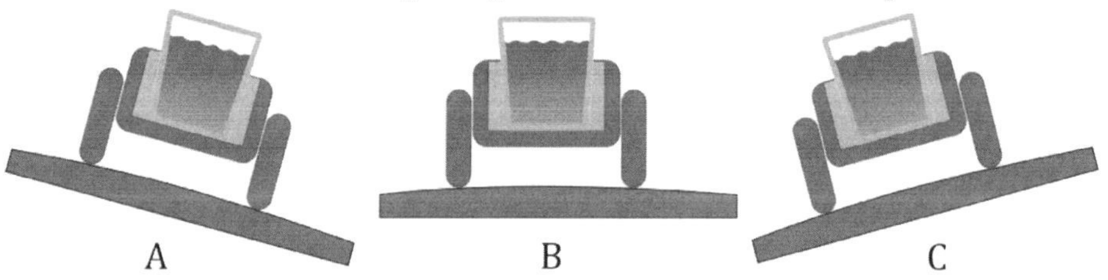

34. Two cars go along the track. Which car travels the greatest distance? (If equal, mark C)

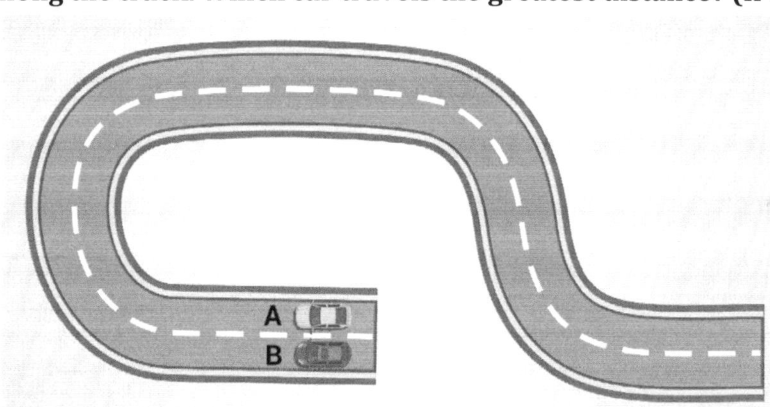

35. Six identical cogs spin each other. If the first is spinning clockwise, which cog is also spinning clockwise?

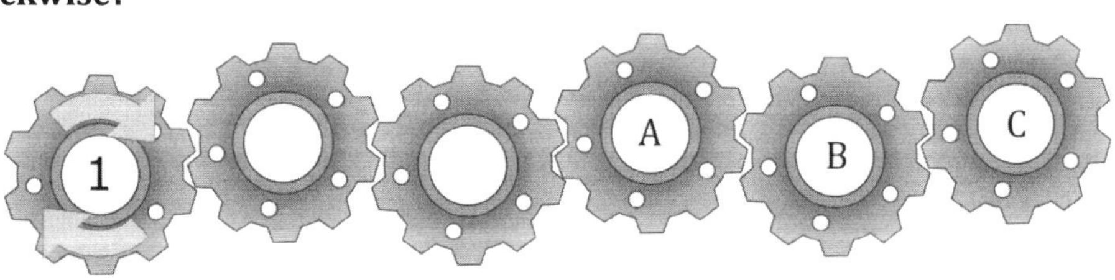

36. Twin goats push each other with their horns. One goat is standing on ice (left), but the other is on dirt (right). Which goat will succeed in pushing the other goat back? (If equal, mark C)

37. A man tries to brace a falling wall. In which position is it best for the man to push?

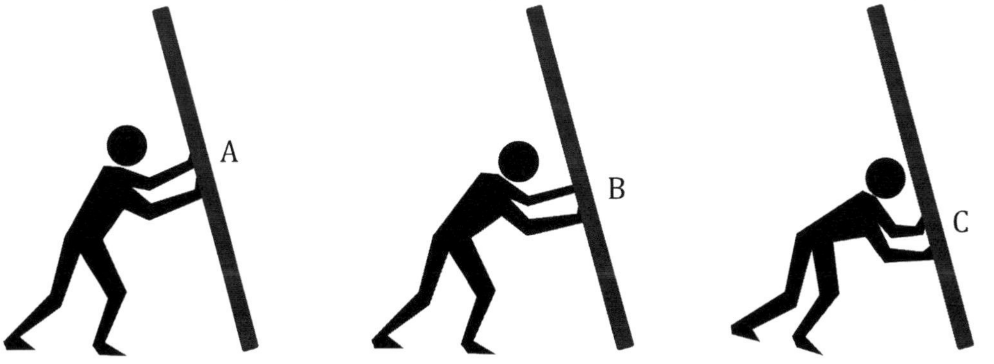

38. Which switch, if opened, guarantees that all the lights in the circuit are turned off?

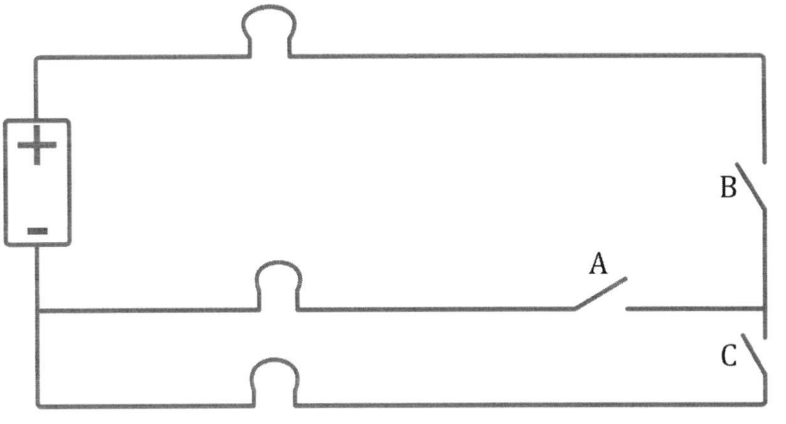

39. Two bowling balls are the same size, but ball B weighs more than ball A. Which ball is more likely to float in a tank of fluid? (If equal, mark C)

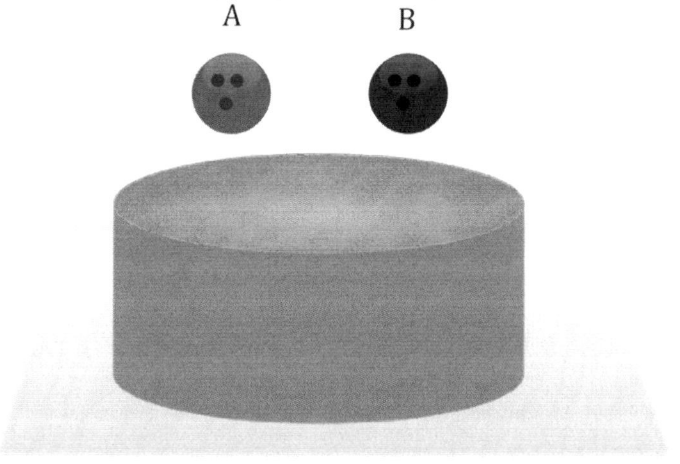

40. Which arrangement of boxes on the cart is more likely to result in tipping? (If equal, mark C)

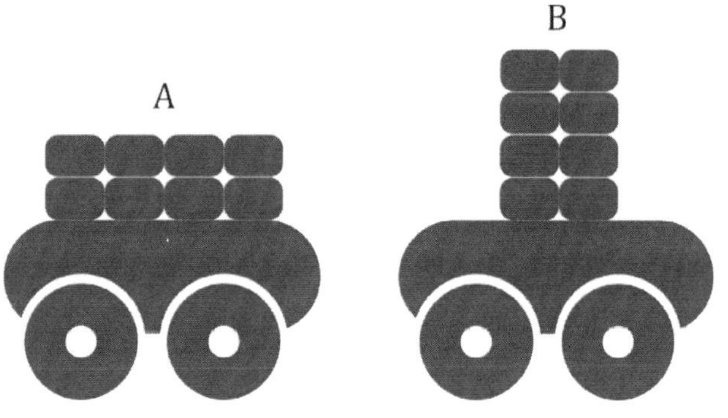

41. Two identical valves have differently sized handwheels. Which handwheel will require the least amount of force to use? (If equal, mark C)

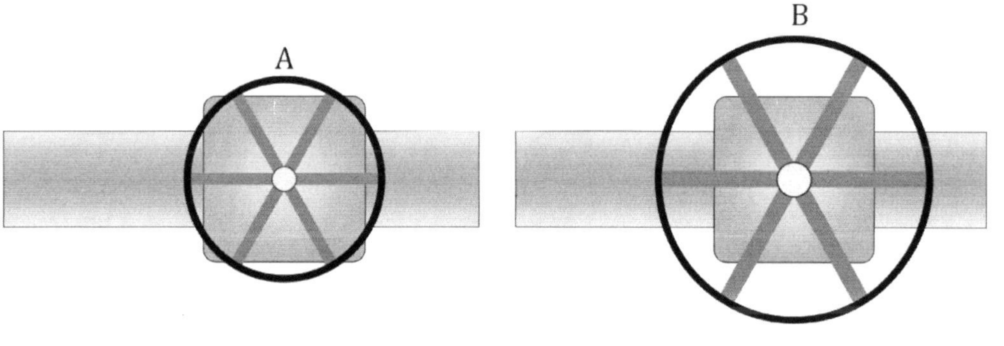

42. Two weights, one forty-pound weight and one eighty-pound weight, are dropped from a height of four feet over the ground. Which weight will hit the ground with more force? (If equal, mark C)

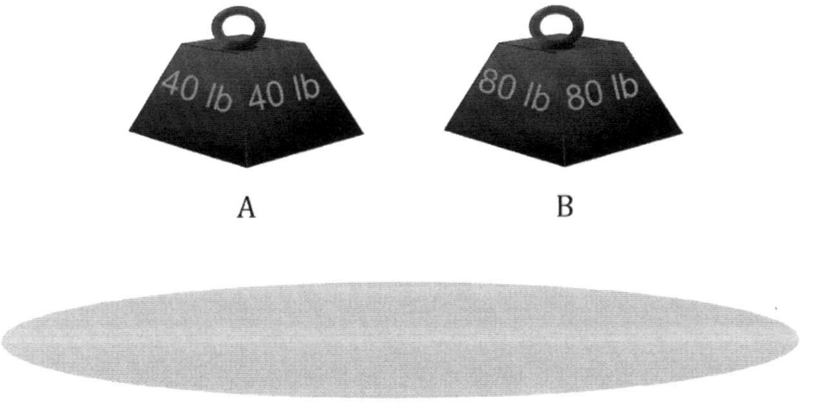

43. A boat is driving in circles. A man on the boat jumps straight up. Where will the man tend to go?

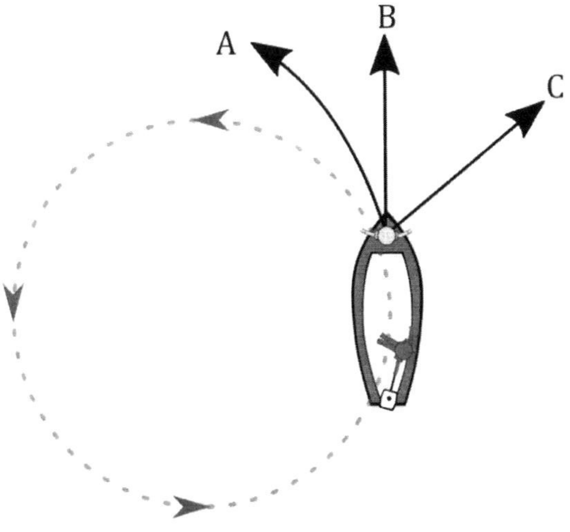

44. A baseball player swings his bat at a specific rotational speed. Where should the ball hit to rebound with the highest speed?

Answers and Explanations

Mathematical Usage

1. D:

$$420 \text{ gallons } \times \frac{1 \text{ barrel}}{42 \text{ gallons}} = 10 \text{ barrels}$$

2. B:

$$\frac{1}{16}\text{kilogram } \times \frac{2.2 \text{ pounds}}{1 \text{ kilogram}} \times \frac{16 \text{ ounces}}{1 \text{ pound}} = 2.2 \text{ ounces}$$

3. A:

$$2.2 \text{ pounds} \times \frac{1 \text{ kilogram}}{2.2 \text{ pounds}} \times \frac{1{,}000 \text{ grams}}{1 \text{ kilogram}} = 1{,}000 \text{ grams}$$

4. A:

$$7.2 \text{ kilograms} \times \frac{1 \text{ slug}}{14.59 \text{ kilograms}} = 0.493 \text{ slugs}$$

5. B:

$$2{,}450 \text{ centimeters} \times \frac{1 \text{ meter}}{100 \text{ centimeters}} \times \frac{1 \text{ kilometer}}{1{,}000 \text{ meters}} = 0.0245 \text{ kilometers}$$

6. A:

$$720 \text{ acres} \times \frac{1 \text{ square mile}}{640 \text{ acres}} = 1.125 \text{ square miles}$$

7. D:

$$72 \text{ fathoms} \times \frac{6 \text{ feet}}{1 \text{ fathom}} = 432 \text{ feet}$$

8. B:

$$7.2 \text{ pints} \times \frac{1 \text{ quart}}{2 \text{ pints}} \times \frac{1 \text{ gallon}}{4 \text{ quarts}} = 0.9 \text{ gallons}$$

9. C:

$$8 \text{ quarts} \times \frac{1 \text{ gallon}}{4 \text{ quarts}} \times \frac{3.785 \text{ liters}}{1 \text{ gallon}} = 7.57 \text{ liters}$$

10. A:

$$0.035 \text{ grams} \times \frac{1 \text{ kilogram}}{1{,}000 \text{ grams}} = 0.000035 \text{ kilograms}$$

11. B:

$$9 \text{ miles/hour} \times \frac{4.4 \text{ feet/second}}{3 \text{ miles/hour}} = 13.2 \text{ feet/second}$$

12. C:

$$15 \text{ kilograms} \times \frac{1 \text{ slug}}{14.59 \text{ kilograms}} \approx 1.03 \text{ slugs}$$

13. B:

$$10{,}560 \text{ feet} \times \frac{1 \text{ mile}}{5{,}280 \text{ feet}} \times \frac{1.609 \text{ kilometers}}{1 \text{ mile}} = 3.218 \text{ kilometers}$$

14. D:

$$3.785 \text{ liters} \times \frac{1 \text{ gallon}}{3.785 \text{ liters}} \times \frac{4 \text{ quarts}}{1 \text{ gallon}} = 4 \text{ quarts}$$

15. C:

$$1{,}500 \text{ grams} \times \frac{1 \text{ kilogram}}{1{,}000 \text{ grams}} \times \frac{2.2 \text{ pounds}}{1 \text{ kilogram}} = 3.3 \text{ pounds}$$

16. D:

$$25.4 \text{ hands} \times \frac{10 \text{ centimeters}}{1 \text{ hand}} \times \frac{1 \text{ inch}}{2.54 \text{ centimeters}} = 100 \text{ inches}$$

17. C:

$$2 \text{ gallons} \times \frac{4 \text{ quarts}}{1 \text{ gallon}} \times \frac{2 \text{ pints}}{1 \text{ quart}} \times \frac{4 \text{ gills}}{1 \text{ pint}} = 64 \text{ gills}$$

18. D:

$$10 \text{ fathoms} \times \frac{6 \text{ feet}}{1 \text{ fathom}} \times \frac{12 \text{ inches}}{1 \text{ foot}} = 720 \text{ inches}$$

Reading for Comprehension

1. A: The passage is a comparison of insulators and conductors.

2. B: In the first paragraph, it states that "almost all metals are excellent conductors."

3. A: This idea is advanced in the fourth sentence of the second paragraph.

4. B: This example is given in the last sentence of the first paragraph.

5. C: This is evident from the first sentence, which begins by noting that "Materials may be classified as insulators or conductors." The rest of the passage describes the behavior and uses of these materials.

6. B: The third sentence of the third paragraph states that selenium is a photoconductor, which the previous sentence has defined as "a material that is an insulator in the dark, but will conduct a charge when light shines upon it."

7. D: This information is given in the first two sentences of the last paragraph.

8. D: The passage describes the operation of steam turbines and the use of steam power plants.

9. A: The fourth sentence of the final paragraph states that steam power plants "usually must be placed near bodies of water." The third sentence of the second paragraph, meanwhile, states that these plants "can be built almost anywhere, which means that they can be positioned strategically to minimize transportation costs." Therefore, of the given answer choices, a large pond alongside a major highway" would be best.

10. B: This definition is given in the second sentence of the second paragraph.

11. A: The second sentence of the second paragraph states explicitly that steam power plants do not require expensive fuel. The other answer choices are real disadvantages and are all mentioned in the third paragraph.

12. B: This article is written in common language, and presumes no special knowledge on the part of the reader. It is too advanced for children, however.

13. C: This sentence suggests that steam power plants may consistently be run at the optimal level, thus eliminating waste.

14. D: This passage describes the various dangers associated with radiation.

15. B: This information is given in the third sentence of the passage. Rem is a measure that takes into account the amount and the type of radiation.

16. A: This fact is given in the last sentence of the second paragraph.

17. D: In the third sentence of the second paragraph, it states that, "People who fly a great deal, or even just live at a high elevation, are more susceptible to radiation originating beyond the earth's atmosphere."

18. C: Radon gas is the subject of the third paragraph.

19. C: This information is given in the second sentence of the third paragraph.

20. B: This is indicated in the second sentence of the third paragraph.

21. A: The second-to-last sentence of the third paragraph addresses this problem. The wide distribution of radon-prone rocks and soils makes it difficult to identify potential dangers.

22. B: The passage describes some of the new methods for reducing the environmental impact of coal power production. It does not focus on the consumer or the ways in which coal impacts the environment.

23. C: The proposed destinations for sequestered carbon are mentioned in the second sentence of the second paragraph.

24. C: This is explicit in the second sentence of the third paragraph.

25. A: The sentence is about methods for diminishing the impact of greenhouse gases.

26. D: This information is given in the second sentence of the third paragraph.

27. D: This definition is given in the second sentence of the fourth paragraph.

28. B: According to the last sentence of the passage, this technology is still in the "trial phase."

29. A: The passage is a comprehensive look at nuclear power plants, including advantages, disadvantages, and site selection.

30. C: The passage names this process in its second sentence.

31. B: The second paragraph of the passage deals primarily with the advantages of nuclear power plants, as is indicated by the first sentence of this paragraph.

32. A: This information is given in the last two sentence of the first paragraph.

33. D: This is mentioned in the third sentence of the second paragraph, where it states that "a nuclear power plant is the most space-efficient type of power plant."

34. A: This reason is mentioned in the last sentence of the second paragraph.

35. B: In the second to last sentence of the third paragraph, the passage states that "there is always the risk of a catastrophic accident at a nuclear power plant."

36. A: This sentence introduces the main idea, and the other sentences provide detail and examples.

Assembling Objects

Question	Answer
1	C
2	B
3	D
4	D
5	A
6	D
7	B
8	C
9	B
10	A
11	D
12	C
13	B
14	D
15	C
16	A
17	D
18	A
19	C
20	A

Mechanical Concepts

1. B: Objects on steeper inclines have less mechanical advantage and require more force to support and lift. Thus, the motor pulling up slope B will need less force. (Think: sliding an object on the floor vs. pulling an object straight up)

2. B: The weight in B is spread across four ropes. Thus, B requires one quarter of the pulling force needed for A.

3. C: These five gears will lock up and not rotate at all because adjacent gears always reverse rotation direction, and this formation would require two adjacent gears to rotate in the same direction.

4. B: The clay on the left has more potential energy from being higher, and will be able to push the other block to the right upon collision.

5. A: Because the same amount of water has to flow through the opening of the funnel as the end of the funnel, the velocity of the water at the exit will be greater.

6. B: Because there is less friction between the slope and the ice, the block on ice will accelerate faster.

7. B: The lowered mass does not change the overall volume. This means that the container will have a lower density and thus a lower pressure.

8. C: Because the outside of all of the pulleys is traveling at the same linear speed, the lowest rotational speed will be the pulley with the largest radius.

9. A: The location farthest from the hinge will provide the greatest moment on the gate to keep it closed.

10. C: Because the ball has the same height when it lands as when it was kicked, it has the same speed as when it was kicked.

11. B: The longer lever requires less force to provide the same amount of torque for lifting the rock.

12. C: Switch C completes the circuit between the battery and the light bulb. Switch B creates a short circuit, and switch A is redundant because there is a parallel path.

13. B: Because the truck is closer to boat B, boat B lifts a greater percentage of the truck and bridge's weight.

14. B: Because the longer machete will cover more area when swung, it will be able to cut more grass per swing, allowing for faster cutting.

15. A: Increasing the density of the water by adding salt makes it more likely that an object will have a density low enough to float.

16. A: Water pressure increases with depth. Adding water will increase the depth, which will therefore increase the pressure at the bottom of the water tower.

17. A: The man will cool down faster with more of the surface area of his body under the water.

18. B: The measuring cup will only be accurate when the milk is parallel to the lines for measuring.

19. B: Car B has a higher center of gravity, making it more unstable than car A.

20. B: The water level will find an equilibrium between the tank and any connected tubes.

21. A: Springs with more compression have more elastic potential energy to convert into kinetic energy and, thus, height.

22. C: Because linear speed increases with radius, the end of the blade will be traveling fastest.

23. B: A greater volume of sand will displace a greater volume of water, and this will present as a higher water level.

24. C: Because the balls are identical in mass and speed, the balls will conserve momentum but exchange direction with the ball they collide with. In this case, ball 1 will rebound off ball 2 in the direction ball 2 was initially traveling. Conversely, ball 2 will follow ball 1's initial path toward the upper right.

25. C: Because the pendulum will lose energy each swing, the pendulum will not be able to go as high as it initially went.

26. A: The board will be easiest to lift when the concrete is farthest from the man.

27. B: The bowling ball at 10 feet has more potential energy to convert into kinetic energy that will compress the spring.

28. A: The constant linear speed applied to roll A will cause it to make more full revolutions in the same amount of time because it has a smaller radius.

29. C: The same amount of water flows through both parts of the pipe. Because the areas are the same, the velocity will be the same.

30. B: In the absence of air resistance, the acceleration of an object in freefall is independent of the object's size, shape, or mass. Thus, both objects will fall at the same rate.

31. B: Once the child lets go of the ball, the ball is not under any external forces and will continue traveling in a straight line tangential to the circular path.

32. A: Because the smaller wheel has to turn more times to cover the same distance as the large wheel, the small wheel will rotate faster.

33. A: On a sharp right curve, the water will tend to spill to the left. Thus, the road should tilt to the right to help the water stay in the bucket.

34. B: Because car A is on the inside of a curve more times than car B, car B travels the greatest distance.

35. B: Because adjacent cogs spin in opposite directions, odd numbered cogs will spin in the same direction. Cog B is the fifth cog, and spins in a clockwise direction.

36. B: The goat on dirt will have more friction force to aid him and will be able to push the other goat back.

37. A: By moving higher up on the wall, the distance from the pivot point is increased which allows for the greatest torque on the wall.

38. B: Opening switch B would prevent the completion of any circuit.

39. A: Because ball A has a smaller mass but the same volume as ball B, it has a lower density, and is therefore more likely to float.

40. B: The center of gravity in truck B is higher, making it more likely to tip.

41. B: Torque increases with radius. Thus, a larger radius would allow a smaller force to achieve the same torque as a smaller radius and a larger force.

42. B: The larger weight has more mass and equivalent acceleration due to gravity. Force is equal to mass multiplied by acceleration, so the weight with more mass will hit with greater force.

43. B: Once the man is off the boat, the man is not under any external forces and will continue traveling in a straight line tangential to the circular path.

44. C: The bat has the greatest linear speed at the farthest point from the center.

It's Your Moment, Let's Celebrate It!

Share your story @mometrixtestpreparation